RICHARD L. STRAUSS
WIN THE BATTLE FOR YOUR MIND

While this book is designed for the reader's personal enjoyment and profit, it is also intended for group study. A Leader's Guide with Victor Multiuse Transparency Masters is available from your local bookstore or from the publisher.

VICTOR BOOKS

a division of SP Publications, Inc.
WHEATON. ILLINOIS 60187

Offices also in Fullerton. California • Whitby, Ontario, Canada • Amersham-on-the-Hill, Bucks, England

Third printing, 1982

Scripture quotations are taken from the *New American Standard Bible* (NASB), © 1960, 1962, 1963, 1968, 1971, 1972, 1973, the Lockman Foundation, La Habra, California. Other versions used are the King James Version and the *New International Version* (NIV), © 1978 by the New York International Bible Society. Portions of Scripture which appear in italics are treated in this manner by the author for emphases. All Scripture used with permission.

Recommended Dewey Decimal Classification: 248.27
Suggested subject headings: CHRISTIAN LIFE; SPIRITUAL DISCIPLINES

Library of Congress Catalog Card Number: 80-51559
ISBN: 0-89693-003-3

VICTOR BOOKS
A division of SP Publications, Inc.
P.O. Box 1825 • Wheaton, Illinois 60187

CONTENTS

To: The faithful folks in
Fort Worth, Texas
Huntsville, Alabama
and
Escondido, California
who have allowed me to serve
as their pastor-teacher
and share with them
the great truths of God's Word.

I
Win
the Battle
for Your Mind

"You don't have a brain in your head!" Would you believe somebody actually said that to me once? As a matter of fact, it has probably been said more than once. But it simply is not true. If a person is alive and functioning, you can be sure he has a brain in his head.

And what an organ it is—an amazingly complex electrical-chemical marvel, weighing only about three pounds, but containing billions of cells that are capable of performing an incredibly enormous work load—generating, receiving, recording, and transmitting energy. Scientists have estimated that after 70 years of activity, a brain may contain nearly 15 trillion separate pieces of information. Thousands upon thousands of thoughts can pass through it every day but the brain never gets tired. It is a magnificent thinking machine with marvelous capacity.

My problem is I never use my brain to its full potential. Most of us seldom use more than 10 percent of the brain's capacity. And that is unfortunate, because the more we use our brains, the more effective they become. Many people testify that the more material they memorize, the easier it is for them to memorize. And obviously, the more we use the brain, the more information it stores up. The brain is a veritable treasure house of memories more vast than we can ever imagine.

But man is more than a machine, and the part of him we call the *mind* goes beyond that lump of gray protein with the consistency of soft cheese located under the skull. Philosophers have quibbled for centuries over the nature of the mind, and we are certainly not going to have the last word here. Most everyone would agree that the functions of the mind do depend to a large degree on the memory storehouse of the brain, and that the thinking processes of the mind are obviously centered in the brain, but the concept of mind does seem to reach in a broader sense to something beyond those processes. It somehow relates to the entire immaterial part of man's being.

While the term *mind* is sometimes used to refer merely to our intellectual faculties, it is likewise used to refer to that whole complex of elements in us that feels, perceives, thinks, wills, and reasons. The mind is the control center of our being where the basic direction of our lives is established. What goes on there determines what we are and what we shall become. The information received there, the experiences encountered there, and the conditioning that takes place there all affect the decisions we make and the course of action we take. Three thousand years ago Solomon wrote, "For as he thinks within himself, so he is" (Prov. 23:7). The things that go on in our minds are the raw materials from which our entire lives are molded.

We can understand, then, why the mind would become a battleground. Everybody who wants us to agree with him about anything, or wants to get something out of us, or wants us to act in some particular way, will try to manipulate us by feeding his own slanted information into our minds. Madison Avenue advertising men, politicians of various stripes, advocates of varied philosophies and lifestyles, assorted religious organizations, and others are all trying to get a foot in the door of our minds and mold our thinking. It is no surprise that mental turmoil abounds and mental disorders skyrocket. Our minds are being pulled in every direction and, oftentimes, we simply do not know whom to believe.

There is an answer to our dilemma. It is to tune our minds to the right channel and get our information from the only completely accurate and authoritative source—the inspired Word of God. Listening to what God has to say will clear up our confusion and help us get our heads on straight. Let's see what God says about our minds.

The Condition of the Natural Mind

God created Adam with a mind. He had the ability to think, reason, and understand, as well as to perceive, to feel, and to will. The evidence is unmistakable. Adam named every species of beast and fowl on the earth of his day (Gen. 2:19-20), and that took some mammoth mental powers. He understood his responsibility to have dominion over the earth (Gen. 1:28). He learned to till the soil and to care for the garden in which God placed him (Gen. 2:15). He was able to comprehend God's plan for marriage and to love his wife (Gen. 2:23-24).

His descendants likewise showed advanced mental development. His son Abel acquired the necessary techniques to raise sheep successfully (Gen. 4:2). Some of his descendants through Cain demonstrated unusual musical talent (Gen. 4:21). Others had the ability to forge all kinds of tools out of bronze and iron (Gen. 4:22). One of his descendants through Seth gave particular attention to cultivating a close personal relationship with the Lord. "And Enoch walked with God" (Gen. 5:24). That was the major reason God made human beings with minds, so that they could get to know Him, enter into a mutually satisfying relationship with Him, enjoy His fellowship, and glorify Him. God would receive great glory from created beings with vast mental capacities choosing to know and worship Him.

But something happened very early in man's history. Rather than seeking to glorify his Creator, the first man chose to defy Him. He ate of the forbidden tree of the knowledge of good and evil and something happened to his mind. For the first time since he had been created, he *knew* evil. His mind became familiar with and affected by sin. And since the immaterial part of Adam's being was passed on to his children, their minds were also affected by sin from the very day of their birth. From Adam's time to this, the mind of every person born into the world has been influenced by sin. Scripture has quite a bit to say about the condition of the natural mind, the mind with which we have been born.

First of all, the mind is darkened. "This I say therefore, and affirm together with the Lord, that you walk no longer just as the Gentiles also walk, in the futility of their mind, being darkened in their understanding" (Eph. 4:17-18). That word *understanding* is another term for the mind and is so translated in several passages of Scripture. The unbeliever lives with his mind fixed on futile things, transitory things, things without eternal value. He lacks spiritual discernment. He is in the dark about spiritual matters. He may understand some very intricate things in this world, things like Einstein's theory of relativity or other complicated and sophisticated scientific and technical information, but he is in a fog about God.

At least one person is pleased about man's darkened mind and does everything he can to keep it shaded from spiritual truth. As the Apostle Paul put it, "The god of this age has blinded the minds of unbelievers, so that they cannot see the light of the Gospel of the glory of Christ, who is in the image of God" (2 Cor. 4:4, NIV). The god of this age is Satan, and he is battling to maintain control of men's minds. He will use every weapon in his diversified arsenal to secure these minds for his cause.

Man's will can only choose what his mind has first grasped. His freedom of choice is restricted to the information he has in his mind. So if Satan can keep man's mind shielded from the truth of the Gospel, he effectively keeps man from getting to know God and from fulfilling God's purpose for creating him. Satan keeps man in spiritual darkness.

Second, God says the natural mind is defiled. "To the pure, all things are pure; but to those who are defiled and unbelieving, nothing is pure, but both their mind and their conscience are defiled. They profess to know God, but by their deeds they deny Him, being detestable and disobedient, and worthless for any good deed" (Titus 1:15-16). Here are people who say they know God, but their manner of living exposes a certain phoniness to their words. Paul says their minds are defiled. The word *defiled* originally meant to dye with another color, but came also to refer to staining, soiling, polluting, or contaminating. We can see the evidence of such mental pollution all around us in a multiplying morass of immorality and licentiousness.

It is actually possible for Satan to pump his defilement right into the unguarded believer's home via television. There is much concern these days about air and water pollution, as there well should be. But one of our primary concerns as Christians ought to be mind pollution—the effects of unbelievers' defiled minds on our lives, the impact of their obscenities, blasphemies, impurities, and unbiblical concepts on our children through the media.

Some unbelievers seem to have garbage cans for minds, and they scatter their moral muck every time they open their mouths. There are some wholesome and profitable programs on television which I watch periodically. But I am astounded at what I allow to enter my mind in the process before I even realize what is happening. And the danger is not only from immorality and profanity. Every natural mind is polluted with misinformation about God, soiled with false doctrine and erroneous ideas that affect aims, attitudes, and actions.

Third, the natural mind is depraved. Paul spoke about "men of depraved mind and deprived of the truth, who suppose that godliness is a means of gain" (1 Tim. 6:5). The word *depraved* means basically corrupted, destroyed, ruined, spoiled, or debased. Those perverted men of Paul's day were teaching that the primary purpose of religion was to raise one's social status and increase one's net worth. They were obviously deficient in truth and could not accomplish anything spiritually profitable. That is not to imply that unbelievers can never say anything good or true. They may think nice thoughts, write great music or poetry, and otherwise make a constructive contribution to mankind. But they are incapable of producing anything that makes them acceptable to an infinitely holy God. Men of depraved minds are "rejected as regards the faith" (2 Tim. 3:8).

Finally, the natural mind is dead. "For the mind set on the flesh is death, but the mind set on the Spirit is life and peace, because the mind set on the flesh is hostile toward God; for it does not subject itself to the law of God, for it is not even able to do so" (Rom. 8:6-7). This mind set on the flesh is the natural mind, the mind with which we were born, with all its sinful inclinations. It is dead, spiritually dead, separated from the life of God. It may function adequately in other spheres. It may invent spectacular new gadgets to make a better life on earth, or initiate philanthropic and humanitarian plans to help underprivileged people. But the natural mind is unable to function toward God, to know God, or to have fellowship with God, and, consequently, is unable to fulfill the purpose for which it was made. The unregenerate mind is actually an enemy of God; it is estranged from the living God; it is spiritually dead (cf. Col. 1:21).

We do not hear many experts on the mind telling us what God says. Most of them are trying to convince us that man's mind is inherently good, that there are no limits to its capabilities, that adequate training is all that it needs. Evidence is even being presented to prove that the mind can accomplish supernatural things apart from outside supernatural intervention, such as moving objects without force, obtaining information apart from the senses, and projecting itself into other time frames and places. I cannot pass judgment on what man's mind is capable of producing or not producing, but I do know that Satan would like to convince us that man's mind is all-sufficient and supreme in itself, that it can solve all of our problems by its own sheer genius, and that it has no need for God.

Man's mind is great! There is no question about that. There

has never been a computer built that can match its capabilities. But the mind is also darkened, defiled, depraved, and spiritually dead. And we need to recognize this if we want our minds to be delivered from their natural, sinful condition and to fulfill God's purpose for their creation.

The Cure for the Natural Mind

There is a remedy for this mental malady. It is not throwing our brains to the breeze as some professing Christians would have us believe. They say Christianity is inconsistent with man's reason, that Christianity is basically irrational: "Don't try to understand it; just take a blind leap of faith and believe it." There are others who would never admit they believe Christianity is irrational, but their actions would seem to imply that they do. Their approaches are purely emotional and their innuendos are clearly anti-intellectual. They may appeal to people to believe the Gospel and make a decision, but they seldom define what the Gospel is or explain what needs to be decided. And they may even ridicule those who apply themselves diligently to an accurate understanding and exposition of the Bible's content.

That is a tragic parody of true Christianity. Faith without content is really no faith at all. God doesn't tell us to turn off our brains before we open our Bibles. In fact, the very opposite is true. In order to salvage our minds for His eternal enjoyment and usefulness, God actually works through our minds. Jesus said we would *know* the truth, and the truth would make us free (John 8:32). He was telling us that there are some things we need to know in order to be released from our sin-sickness and Satanic blindness. And the only way we will ever be free to turn to God is to get that information into our minds. Since the mind is the control center of the life, and since it is so dreadfully sick, God through His Spirit puts particular emphasis on it as He applies His divine medication. He does this basically in three ways:

First, He convinces us of our need. Shortly before He left the earth, Jesus said to His diciples, "I tell you the truth, it is to your advantage that I go away; for if I do not go away, the Helper shall not come to you; but if I go, I will send Him to you. And He, when He comes, will convict the world concerning sin, and righteousness, and judgment" (John 16:7-8). The word *convict* means to bring something to light, to point it out and demonstrate it to be true to *convince* someone. It is an action that relates unmistakably to the mind. God the Holy Spirit works on the unbelievers' minds to convince them of three things: sin, righteousness, and judgment. Each one is explained in the verses that follow.

For one thing, He convinces them concerning *sin*; Jesus said ". . . because they do not believe in Me" (John 16:9). Sinners need to be convinced that they have sinned, and that their sin is an affront to a holy God. But notice why it is an affront—because they do not believe in Christ. A sinner does not need to be convinced of sin merely because he cheated on his income tax, or lied to his boss, or angrily screamed at his kids, or committed adultery, or got drunk. He needs to be convinced of his sin because he has not done the one thing that can deliver him from his darkness, defilement, depravity, and spiritual death. He has not placed his trust in the Lord Jesus Christ as the One who paid the penalty for his sins.

Therefore, you see, our problem is not just that we have sinned, but that we have sinned and have not availed ourselves of God's provision for that sin, the death of His Son. We have not trusted Him for forgiveness. And it is that one sin, our failure to place our confidence and trust in His shed blood, that condemns us to eternal separation from God (John 3:18). We need to understand that and accept it. And the Holy Spirit is the One who convinces us.

The second thing Jesus said the Holy Spirit convinces us of is righteousness; "Because I go to the Father, and you no longer behold Me" (John 16:10). What does it mean to convince us of righteousness? If we were truly righteous, we would hardly need to be convinced of it. Our problem is that we have the wrong kind of righteousness. We have tried to offer God our own righteousness and have not received the perfect righteousness which He offers us in response to our faith (cf. Rom. 10:3). We think our righteousness is sufficient to gain us entrance into heaven, but God says it is inadequate. In fact, He says our righteous deeds are like filthy rags (Isa. 64:6). And our minds can never be delivered from the natural condition until we become convinced of our unrighteousness and of the need for Christ's righteousness to be credited to us by faith.

Why does the Holy Spirit need to convince us about true righteousness? Because Christ has gone to the Father. When Christ was on earth, His perfect righteousness was obvious for all to see if they looked at Him with open minds. His righteousness exposed their unrighteousness and made them see their need to receive His imputable (transferable) righteousness. But now He has gone back to the Father. We cannot see Him. And since He is not physically present, it is easy for some to say that He is an imposter, a liar, a sinful man who can hardly help any of us obtain the necessary righteousness. But the Holy Spirit gives testimony to His sinlessness, His infinite righteousness. He convinces us that Christ is the perfect Son of God who offers to transfer (impute) His righteousness to our account when we put our trust in Him. We need to acknowledge that there is no other way to be fit for God's presence, and the Holy Spirit is trying to persuade us of that.

The third thing the Holy Spirit convinces us of is judgment; Jesus said, ". . . because the ruler of this world has been judged" (John 16:11). The whole concept of judgment for sin is the laughingstock of the unbelieving world. "Look how much I've gotten away with," some boast. "Besides, if there is a God, He's a God of love. He wouldn't condemn anyone to hell." God *is* loving! But He is also holy and just, and those attributes require Him to judge sin. We know He will do it too, because He has already judged Satan.

Satan judged? That confuses some people. How can he give us so much trouble if he has already been judged? Shortly before He died, Jesus said, "Now the ruler of this world shall be cast out" (John 12:31). When Christ died on that cross,

Satan's doom was assured. His sentence was pronounced and his days are numbered. And those who reject Jesus Christ will share Satan's doom. Their judgment is just as certain as Satan's is. Someday Christ will say to them, "Depart from Me, you who are cursed, into the eternal fire prepared for the devil and his angels" (Matt. 25:41, NIV). That is not a pleasant thought, but it makes sense. A perfectly holy God could not leave sin and rebellion unpunished. He will judge! We need to understand that and believe it, and the Holy Spirit is the One who convinces us.

Sometimes the Holy Spirit uses people. He used the Apostle Paul, for example, when he arrived in Thessalonica on his second missionary journey. "As his custom was, Paul went into the synagogue, and on three Sabbath days he *reasoned* with them from the Scriptures, *explaining* and *proving* that the Christ had to suffer and rise from the dead" (Acts 17:2-3, NIV). That was obviously an appeal to the mind. And God used it mightily. "Some of the Jews were *persuaded* and joined Paul and Silas, as did a large number of God-fearing Greeks and not a few prominent women" (Acts 17:4, NIV). The Spirit of God can employ a believer whom He controls to give a clear, intelligent, and logical presentation of the Gospel which will capture the minds of unbelievers and convince them of their need for Christ.

There is something else which the Spirit of God does to our minds in order to deliver them from their natural condition. After He convinces us of our need, *He challenges us to repent.* Paul summed this up in his famous sermon on Mars Hill in Athens. "In the past God overlooked such ignorance, but now He commands all people everywhere to repent" (Acts 17:30, NIV). The word translated "repent" is actually composed of two Greek words, one of which is the word for the mind. It means, literally, "to think afterward" or "to change the mind."

What is it about which we are to change our minds? The word *repentance* is linked to several key issues in Scripture. For one thing there is repentance toward God (Acts 20:21). I do not know what you think about God, but if it is anything other than what He reveals about Himself in His Word, then you need to change your mind. The Bible portrays Him as a holy Being who hates sin, but also as a loving Being who Himself has provided for the sinner's forgiveness in the death of His Son. Is that the way you view Him? If not, He wants you to change your mind.

Several passages link repentance to sin (e.g., Acts 8:22). Some people will insist, "But my sins aren't so bad. They're no worse than anyone else's. Besides, everyone is entitled to a few, isn't he?" That is exactly what we need to change our minds about. We need to admit that every sin, no matter how small, is contrary to everything God is. It is an offense to His holiness, a challenge to His authority, and a just cause for our eternal condemnation.

"But I've done a lot of good deeds in my life. They count for something, don't they?" That is another thing about which we must change our minds. Repentance from dead works (Heb. 6:1) is a reference to religious rituals and ceremonies. There is nothing wrong with religious observances, unless they become empty, meaningless routines, or unless we think we are buying some special privileges from God by performing them. All the good deeds of a lifetime cannot erase the consequences of one sin or move us one inch closer to heaven (cf. Titus 3:5; Eph. 2:8-9). If we do not believe that, God challenges us to change our minds.

Finally, repentance is linked to the Person of Jesus Christ (Acts 3:18-19). The Bible presents Him as God the Son, who left the realm of eternity to visit our planet, who lived a sinless life, who died a sacrificial death in our place, and then who arose triumphant over sin and the grave to secure our eternal salvation. And He said that He is the only way to the Father (John 14:6). It may require some changes in our thinking to acknowledge that. But when we trust Him as personal Saviour from the guilt and condemnation of sin, God promises to save us (Acts 16:31), that is, to deliver us from the penalty which our sins justly deserve. Then He releases our minds from Satan's grasp, and from their darkness, defilement, depravity, and death. In place of darkness, He gives light. In place of defilement, He brings cleansing. In place of depravity, He allows eternal usefulness. In place of death, He imparts eternal life. And He opens our minds to whole new realms of spiritual truth.

2
The Enemy
of the Mind

Wouldn't it be nice if Satan left us alone after we got saved? You might think he would have no more interest in us. We are lost to him for eternity. He can never lay claim to us again. Yet he never seems to get off our case. Why is that? It's because he has discovered that he can do just as much damage to the cause of Christ by influencing a Christian's mind as he can by totally controlling an unbeliever's mind.

When a person trusts Christ as Saviour, something happens to his mind. God gives it new capacities. Whereas before his mind was darkened by sin, God now cleanses and illuminates it with spiritual truth. Whereas before his mind was spiritually dead, God now gives it the ability to know Him and please Him. He does not actually give this new Christian a second mind, making him spiritually schizoid, but God does place within his mind the new capability of serving and pleasing Him. For all practical purposes, we can call it a new mind. It is a mind capable of accomplishing the original purpose for its creation—fellowshiping with God and giving glory to Him.

The Conflict in the Believer's Mind
Having a new mind creates some problems, however, for while the believing mind has new capacities, it does not lose its old

capacity for sin. A struggle is in progress. On the one hand there is an inclination toward God; on the other, an inclination toward sin. The Apostle Paul described the conflict as it raged in his own mind: "But I see another law in my members, warring against the law of my mind, and bringing me into captivity to the law of sin which is in my members. . . . So then with the mind I myself serve the law of God; but with the flesh the law of sin" (Rom. 7:23, 25, KJV). On one hand there is the new mind, which Paul called merely "my mind." It longs to do what is right in God's sight. But on the other hand there is the flesh, the old sin nature, the old inclinations of the natural mind which is longing to do what is contrary to God's will.

Now Satan knows this doctrine. He never went to seminary, but he knows more theology than all the world's seminary professors put together. He has had thousands of years to learn this doctrine, and he uses all of it to his own advantage. He appeals to the flesh (the old mind) through the ungodly world system, and by it tries to lure us away from doing the will of God (cf. 1 John 2:15-17). If he can succeed, he substantially stifles the work of God in the world, because God has chosen to do His work primarily through us, His people. And there is a distinct possibility that he will succeed. Paul expressed that fear regarding the Corinthians: "But I am afraid that just as Eve was deceived by the serpent's cunning, your minds may somehow be led astray from your sincere and pure devotion to Christ" (2 Cor. 11:3, NIV).

So the battle for our minds goes on even after salvation. And what a crucial battle it is! The sad thing is that some Christians do not even realize they are in a battle. Satan brainwashes them so subtly, they they don't know it is happening. They are slowly and systematically saturated with the world's philosophy and stripped of any effective usefulness to the Saviour—and they never even suspect it is happening.

Satan's approaches are legion, for he is the great deceiver (Rev. 12:9). He uses *wiles*, or tricky schemes (Eph. 6:11). He employs *devices*, carefully designed plots (2 Cor. 2:11).

And his goal is to devour us, that is to swallow us up in sin and destroy our testimony (1 Peter 5:8).

One of his most successful methods is through the use of the media. He plants thoughts in our minds daily through television, radio, newspapers, magazines, books, motion pictures, and billboards. He is particularly effective in getting us bogged down in the quagmire of materialism by this means, as we shall see in a later chapter. He also finds the media useful for slipping his standards of morality into our minds. Most of us know that the Bible teaches sexual purity and marital faithfulness, so when somebody comes out and boldly advocates free love, we recognize it as Satan's work. But when we become involved in an emotional, heartwarming story that touches a responsive chord in us, and we identify with the hero's dreams, aspirations, and frustrations, we may suddenly find ourselves cheering him on when he leaves an obnoxious and insensitive wife for a sympathetic and understanding lover. And we may never realize that we have been duped by Satan, softened up to accept the world's values.

Satan is also a master at making us more receptive to false doctrine. "The Spirit clearly says that in later times some will abandon the faith and follow deceiving spirits and things taught by demons" (1 Tim. 4:1, NIV). The ardent devotees of false religious systems say some very reasonable and convincing things, and the way they live sometimes secures for them the admiration of the entire community. But those things are merely Satan's tactics for making their non-biblical views more acceptable. "For such men are false apostles, deceitful workmen, masquerading as apostles of Christ. And no wonder, for Satan himself masquerades as an angel of light. It is not surprising, then, if his servants masquerade as servants of righteousness" (2 Cor. 11:13-15, NIV).

Satan likewise knows the powerful effect of hearing a message repeatedly, over a long period of time, and from many different sources, and he uses that tactic to great advantage. We may hear a newsman say it, then a famous athlete, or a glamorous Hollywood personality, then a leading politician. And when our next-door neighbor, who claims to be a Christian, suggests the same idea, Satan has us hooked.

Our children are being bombarded with erroneous messages not only from the media, but also from their textbooks, their teachers, their friends, and sometimes their friends' parents; and they are in danger of being deluded in matters such as sex, drugs, abortion, marital roles, and divorce. Suddenly, we hear our children saying things like, "Sex before marriage is all right if we have a meaningful relationship," or "Homosexuality is fine if that's the way a person wants to live," or "There's really nothing wrong with marijuana." It can happen to any of us. The sheer weight and persistence of the opposition overwhelms us and wears us down. We do not want to be different or odd, so we give in and then rationalize our surrender with something like, "Well, it *is* possible to interpret those passages in the Bible that way you know."

Music is another powerful mind bender. Those who have studied the effects of contemporary music have found that much of it provides a forceful impetus to accept Satan's world view and promotes the use of harmful drugs and the uninhibited practice of sex, as well as the alienation of the generations.

The immediate impact of Satan's suggestions may not be as damaging as the cumulative effect. Our resistance to temptation does not depend on our spiritual frame of mind at the moment of temptation alone, but also on the attitudes that have been forming in our minds for weeks, or even years, before the temptation occurs. James wrote, "But each one is tempted when he is carried away and enticed by his own lust. Then when lust has conceived, it gives birth to sin; and when sin is accomplished, it brings forth death" (James 1:14-15). There may be a period of time between the conception of lust and the actual birth of sin. If Satan can sow the seeds of unbiblical concepts in our minds by any possible means, and let them incubate, he has laid the foundation for later sin and spiritual defeat. What he can feed into our minds today through the eye-gate and ear-gate will help him accomplish his devious ends tomorrow, or next week, or next year.

Is there any hope of winning this struggle? The odds against us seem to be enormous. We certainly cannot escape every satanic assault, for God has not called us to live in cloistered cells (cf. John 17:15). Is victory then possible? Can we resist Satan's appeal to our sinful natures? Paul wondered the same thing: "O wretched man that I am! Who shall deliver me from the body of this death?" Then he answered his own question: "I thank God through Jesus Christ, our Lord" (Rom. 7:24-25, KJV). Let's see what provision Jesus Christ our Lord has made for victory.

The Conquest by the New Mind

The first thing that should be of help to us in our struggle with Satan is *an understanding of the Christian's armor*. One piece is especially designed to protect the mind, the only piece worn on the head. In order to win this battle with Satan, we must wear "the helmet of salvation" (Eph. 6:17). And it is no accident that the helmet is labeled *salvation*. When we are enjoying the assurance of our salvation, it is difficult for Satan to penetrate our minds. Our response to his attacks will be, "You can't touch me, Satan. I'm a child of God. I have supernatural resources to resist you." And such resistance sends Satan fleeing (James 4:7). When, on the other hand, we are plagued with doubts about our salvation and about the reality of God's work in our lives, then we lower our defenses. We become easy prey for Satan's destructive thoughts.

Have you placed your trust in Jesus Christ as your Saviour from sin? He promised to save you. Take Him at His Word. Don't let Satan tell you anything different. "These things I have written to you who believe in the name of the Son of God, in order that you may *know* that you have eternal life" (1 John 5:13). You can enjoy the assurance of your salvation.

The second important principle for victory is to *be filled with the Spirit*. "And do not get drunk with wine, for that is dissipation, but be filled with the Spirit" (Eph. 5:18). It is unlikely that the role of the Holy Spirit could ever be over-emphasized as a deterrent to Satan's subtle mind-bending strategies. The major point of the Spirit's filling is *control*. Just as alcohol controls the mind of an alcoholic, so the Holy Spirit wants to control our minds. He cannot, of course, until we relinquish that control to Him, yield dominion of our thought processes to Him, and consciously decide that we want His will more than our own will.

The Lord Jesus revealed a significant fact about the Holy Spirit when He called Him *the Spirit of Truth* who would guide us into all truth (John 16:13). If we allow Him to dominate our lives, He can help us sort out truth from error and guard us against Satan's deceptive lies. He can even protect us against Satan's subtle attacks at our weakest points, some which we may not even be aware of. "In the same way, the Spirit helps us in our weakness. We do not know what we ought to pray, but the Spirit Himself intercedes for us with groans that words cannot express" (Rom. 8:26, NIV). He prays for us when we do not know what our needs are, and He stands ready to assist us on a level beyond our conscious awareness. When we are rightly related to the Holy Spirit, Satan cannot make his influence felt on our minds.

A third vital principle for victory is to *be programmed with the Word*. It has been suggested many times that the brain operates much like a computer. Everything we have ever experienced is stored in its memory bank. We cannot always recall this at will, but it is there, permanently filed away for future reference. Neurological surgeons have discovered that by stimulating certain areas of the cortex, patients can relive past incidents, experiencing all the sights, sounds, and sensations of the original events as though they were recorded and played back. All the information which has been fed into our computers through the five senses affects the way we think and the things we do. Jesus said, "But the things that proceed out of the mouth come from the heart, and those defile the man. For out of the heart come evil thoughts, murders, adulteries, fornications, thefts, false witness, slanders" (Matt. 15:18-19).

Those things got into the heart (or mind) primarily through the eye-gate and the ear-gate. Appealing to the old sin nature and reinforcing their hold on the life, these evil thoughts, etc. erupt in sinful words and actions. If Satan can succeed in getting trash fed into our minds, trash is going to pour out from our lives. "Garbage in, garbage out," is the way the computer people put it.

So, what we need to do is to reprogram the "computer" with the Word of God. Filling our minds with God's Word is the only way to erase some of that old satanic input. Jesus said we are clean through the Word (John 15:3). *Clean* is the Greek word from which we get our English word "catharsis," a purification, purgation, or cleansing. God's Word is the only thing that can purge our minds of Satan's crafty suggestions and the world's faulty philosophy. While God's Word may not actually remove Satan's wrong information from our brain cells, it cancels Satan's detrimental effect. The Bible has cleansing power. The psalmist agrees: "How can a young man keep his way pure? By living according to Your Word" (Ps. 119:9, NIV).

The Apostle Paul encouraged us to *renew* our minds (Rom. 12:2). The word he used refers to making something new in the sense of its nature or quality. God wants our minds to be distinctively different from what they were, programmed with His thoughts rather than man's. Whatever else that involves, it certainly requires memorizing the Word, meditating on it, and relating it to our daily living. I am convinced that it is impossible for a Christian to grow in the Lord, to do His will, and to enjoy victory over sin without memorizing and meditating on the Word of God.

As we feed more of the Word into our minds, we are better able to evaluate everything we see and hear from God's perspective. We can test every thought by the standard of the Word, then decide which to discard and which to let settle down and become part of us. The Word provides a major safeguard against Satan's assaults on our minds.

Satan does not like what you are reading right now. He is

trying to bring this concept into disrepute among Christians today. He is trying to get us to bypass our conscious minds and put our trust in a mindless, experience-centered emotionalism. There is a growing distrust in our day of a rational understanding of the Word in favor of an irrational trust in experience. Professing Christians are saying, "I've had this experience, so it must be from God." When we elevate experience over the Word, Satan has us primed for any kind of heretical doctrine or worldly value system he wants to feed in, for he is able to influence and manipulate our experiences. He would love for us to board up our brains and function on emotion and experience alone. Don't do it! Program your mind with God's Word. Study it, learn what it means, memorize it, think about it, and live as it says. God's word is the sword of the Spirit that will send Satan scurrying for cover (cf. Eph. 6: 17).

The last essential principle for victory to consider is this: *Be captivated by Christ.* Paul provided some helpful information to assist us in our struggle with Satan when he said, "For though we walk in the flesh, we do not war according to the flesh" (2 Cor. 10:3). This battle cannot be won with natural resources, with human wisdom, or with the energy of the flesh. We cannot defeat human reason with human reason. Paul went on to explain that the only effective weapons for pulling down Satan's deeply entrenched philosophies are the mighty weapons which God makes available (v. 4). Then he made this penetrating observation: "We are destroying speculations and every lofty thing raised up against the knowledge of God, and we are taking every thought captive to the obedience of Christ" (v. 5). Paul was out to capture for Christ the thoughts of the false apostles at Corinth, but he knew he could only do this as his own thoughts were first brought into submissive obedience to Christ. He was suggesting that we can withstand Satan's reasonings and defeat all the proud ideas that are contrary to the knowledge of God as we subjugate our minds to the obedience of Christ. Paul wanted every thought that lingered in his mind to be at

Christ's command, absolutely subject to Christ, as a war captive is subject to his captor.

But do not miss that word *obedience*. It means, literally, "to hear under." As captives of Christ, under His authority, and as captives fully committed to obey Him, we need to hear every thought that invades our minds. With that decision made, Satan's efforts to influence us with his philosophies and with the world's values will fall on deaf ears. We will be saying, "I can't respond to that. I'm a captive of Christ. I am committed to obey Him."

Most of us long to have good feelings about our lives and about our relationships with other people, but we fail to recognize that obedience is essential to right feelings. We usually have it backward. We say, "If I could feel properly about this, then I would act properly." For example, we may insist, "If I could love my mate more, then I could treat him/her with more respect." Or, "If I could love my children more, I would be more calm and gentle with them." So we pray for more love, and usually get no answer because God has laid down certain prerequisites for enjoying right feelings. But because our feelings have not changed, we get discouraged and defeated, and we blame God for not answering our prayers. The first thing we need to do in a situation like that is to study God's Word to see how love *acts,* then program our minds with that information. When a difficult situation arises, we need to check our first reaction, play the tape of God's Word in our minds, and then consciously choose to act as the Word of God instructs, no matter how we feel.

When we step out by faith to act, God's power and grace become available to help us, and we begin to establish new habit patterns of obedience. They become ingrained in our minds, like rivulets in a hillside during a rain. And right feelings will follow just as surely as God is Truth. Jesus told us to keep His commandments and our joy would be full (John 15:10-11). Try it. Bring every thought captive to the obedience of Christ. Satan's most concentrated and clever tactics to capture your mind will then be frustrated.

3
The Mind
of Christ

As we have seen, the believer has a fourfold blockade against Satan's encroachment into his mind. It involves an assurance of his salvation, a willingness to let the Holy Spirit dominate his life, a mental saturation with the Word of God, and a dedicated determination to obey the Lord. The Apostle Paul has some things to say about a Christian who has been using these resources, and he gives him a title—"he who is spiritual" (1 Cor. 2:15). And spiritual believers, he says, "have the mind of Christ" (v. 16).

The mind of Christ—what does that mean? It certainly does not imply that a spiritually minded Christian can understand every thought that Jesus has. The same writer, addressing the same people, admitted that, rather than fully understanding all spiritual truth, they now know only in part (1 Cor. 13:12). But it does imply that a spiritual Christian is learning to see things from a different perspective than the world sees them. He is beginning to see things from Christ's standpoint. He has a divine outlook rather than a human outlook. He is unlearning the mind-set of the world and learning God's viewpoint on the issues of life. And that is no easy task.

The Spirit of God does offer us some help, however, by

giving several specific examples of the mind of Christ. In each case, Christ's perspective is shockingly different from our perspective. Let me show you what I mean. The most notable passage is one written to the Philippians: "Let this mind be in you, which was also in Christ Jesus" (Phil. 2:5, KJV). That verse introduces the most graphic description of Christ's voluntary self-abasement found anywhere in the New Testament. But it likewise sums up the preceding verses which speak not only of humility, but also of harmony. The mind of Christ is both a harmonious mind and a humble mind.

The Harmonious Mind

Disunity, dissension, and discord are major characteristics of Christians who are operating according to their fleshly minds. Paul had accused some of the Corinthians of being fleshly Christians rather than spiritual Christians with the mind of Christ (1 Cor. 2:16—3:2). Then he said, "For since there is jealousy and strife among you, are you not fleshly, and are you not walking like mere men?" (1 Cor. 3:3) To have a fleshly mind is to experience contention; to have the mind of Christ is to enjoy unity and harmony with others who likewise have the mind of Christ. And that was exactly what Paul desired for all of his converts.

Oneness is clearly emphasized in the Book of Philippians. It is stated several times throughout the epistle. "Only conduct yourselves in a manner worthy of the Gospel of Christ; so that whether I come and see you or remain absent, I may hear of you that you are standing firm in one spirit, with one mind striving together for the faith of the Gospel" (Phil. 1:27). *One spirit* refers to oneness in the deepest part of their being. *One mind* literally means one soul, which includes the intellect, the emotions, and the will. *Striving together* means striving in concert as in an athletic contest, like a tug of war. What a beautiful exhortation to unity!

Then in the central passage on the mind of Christ, Paul wrote, "Make my joy complete by being of the same mind, maintaining the same love, united in spirit, intent on one purpose" (Phil. 2:2). *Being of the same mind* means to keep on thinking the same things. *United in spirit* translates a word that means, literally, fellow-souled; that is, having a harmonious attitude. And in addition to that, they were to be "intent on one purpose," having their minds fixed on the same goals.

He said it over and over again in different ways, but the message was always the same—spiritually minded Christians should be in unity, harmony, agreement, and accord. And when they were not, they needed to be encouraged to resolve their disagreements, as in the case of two women in the church at Philippi: "I urge Euodia and I urge Syntyche to live in harmony in the Lord" (Phil. 4:2). They had evidently allowed misunderstandings and dissension to fester between them; and Paul exhorted them with words that mean, literally, "to think the same things."

We live in a democratic society where the free expression of thought is a cherished privilege. We consider the right of political dissent a necessary part of the system, and the interchange of opposing viewpoints provides a healthy check and balance that keeps extreme elements from dominating our lives. That is a good thing for our society. And since it is good in the political arena, we assume that it will also be good in the spiritual arena; so we transplant the whole concept into our church life. Consequently, some people in the church feel obligated to question every statement, differ with every opinion, and challenge every decision. They may sow seeds of dissension on an individual level, prolong and disrupt board meetings, or plunge congregational meetings into utter chaos. They justify their actions by claiming they want every side to be represented. And when they are asked why, they may answer, "Just for the sake of argument."

I can find no scriptural evidence for every side being represented. And the Holy Spirit never condones anything just for the sake of argument. Arguing is condemned in Scripture! "And the Lord's bond-servant must not be quarrelsome, but be kind to all, able to teach, patient when wronged" (2 Tim. 2:24). Trace the history of the early church that rocked the world with the Gospel of Jesus Christ and you will find people who were of one accord. Four times a word was used that indicated they did things with one mind, or *unanimously* (Acts 1:14; 2:46; 4:24; 5:12). That same word was used in Paul's epistle to the Romans: "Now may the God who gives perseverance and encouragement grant you to be of the same mind with one another according to Christ Jesus; that with one accord you may with one voice glorify the God and Father of our Lord Jesus Christ" (Rom. 15:5-6).

This is not an isolated idea tucked away in one obscure verse. It is an emphasis that permeates the entire New Testament. For example, to the Corinthians Paul said, "Now I exhort you, brethren, by the name of our Lord Jesus Christ, that you all agree, and there be no divisions among you, but you be made complete in the same mind and in the same judgment" (1 Cor. 1:10). That word *judgment* can mean not only purpose or intention, but also *opinion*. Those Christians at Corinth were to have the same opinion on things (cf. also Rom. 12:16; 2 Cor. 13:11; 1 Peter 3:8). The truth is well established—as amazing as it may seem to us—Christians ought to do things with complete agreement. It may be out of step with the way we operate in our secular society, but it is the way things ought to be done in the church of Jesus Christ and in our Christian homes. God wants us to have the same opinion on things.

Now that does raise an obvious question. Should we uncritically accept everything that is stated in our hearing? No, that is not what Scripture is saying. We need not assume that any one person is always right. But the Spirit of God is always right; and when He makes His mind known, we must all say, "Yes, I agree with that." The Holy Spirit cannot contradict Himself. He never has two opposing opinions on the same subject. So we do not need to know every side; we only need to know His side. And it stands to reason that when we all know His mind and accept it, we will all agree.

The first question we must always ask ourselves is, "Does the Spirit of God speak to this issue in the Word?" If He does, then the issue is settled.

We may not all agree at first. We may have to pray together, search the Word together, and discuss the issue together graciously before we can come to a meeting of the minds. That is what happened at the Jerusalem Council. Not all of them agreed when they first started. They called the meeting to resolve their differences over the status of Gentile believers. "But certain ones of the sect of the Pharisees who had believed, stood up, saying, 'It is necessary to circumcise them, and to direct them to observe the Law of Moses'" (Acts 15:5). The narrative goes on to describe the debate that followed. James appealed to the Scriptures (cf. vv. 15-18), and the result was that the Spirit of God brought them to one accord. At the conclusion of the meeting, they were able to write, "It seemed good to us, having become of one mind, to select men to send to you" (Acts 15:25).

If you and I as believers cannot agree on some spiritual issue, then one of us has not yet found the mind of the Spirit—and it is possible that neither of us has. We may need to back up, pray some more, and study the Word together with greater diligence. But prayerfully seeking the mind of the Spirit is entirely different from speaking our mind, or taking the other side for the sake of argument, or disagreeing just to provide a check and balance. The Holy Spirit will provide His own balance. We simply need to know His mind. If our motive for speaking out is to voice our own opinion rather than to help discover the mind of the Spirit, then we ought to be quiet.

If this kind of agreement is possible, some are surely wondering why there have been so many differing opinions on so many spiritual issues throughout the centuries. Why are there so many different denominations with contradictory doctrines today? Why are so many Christian homes in such turmoil? The fact of the matter is that we all have personal biases, prejudices, and preconceived notions which we are unwilling to admit, and which we sometimes do not even recognize. We say we want the mind of the Spirit, but we find it difficult to keep from interjecting our own personal preferences and trying to convince others of our own point of view.

Another problem is that few of us are willing to come together to pray, to study, to share, and to seek the mind of the Holy Spirit with open hearts—and to wait patiently until He makes His mind known. Pastors may not be willing to listen to others in the congregation, nor they to their pastors. Parents may not be willing to listen to their children's point of view, nor children to their parents'. It is obviously not even *possible* for the whole church of Jesus Christ worldwide to come together for dialogue. And God in His grace is pleased to use us in spite of our differences. He used both Paul and Barnabas even though the disagreement between them was sharp on one occasion (Acts 15:39). The contention was not right, but our sovereign God blessed them and their ministries in spite of it.

It may not even be possible for one entire congregation to come to total agreement, since there are in most congregations a mixture of baby Christians, carnal Christians, and others who are not able or not willing to spend the necessary time to resolve the conflict. But it should be possible for the spiritual leaders of a local church to agree. And how much more readily will the rest of the congregation submit to the spiritual leaders as they were commanded to do in the New Testament (Heb. 13:17), if they are assured that the leadership is of one mind. And it is possible for parents and teenagers to sit down together, and calmly share their feelings with one another, search the Word together with open hearts, and come to agreement. How much happier our homes would then be!

Each group of believers must apply this principle to their own situation. It certainly does not permit a selfishly motivated minority in a church to tyrannize the majority by demanding unanimity, then using their negative input to thwart the will of the majority. But the fact remains, the Holy Spirit inspires neither *Roberts Rules of Order* nor majority rule. He brings spiritually minded people to complete agreement. Though the people of the world can never operate this way, since they have no unifying factor, we can, for we have the mind of Christ.

A Humble Mind

What is it that keeps us from enjoying a greater spirit of unity with other Christians? The answer to that question is not very pleasant to face, but we must face it squarely if we want to have the mind of Christ. Our problem is usually our selfishness and pride. Because of our pride, we are often convinced that we are right; so we insist on having our own way, we seek to assert our own rights, we try to control other people, we grasp power for ourselves, and we endeavor to enhance our own image. And that is why the Apostle Paul immediately followed up his encouragement to harmony with this incisive exhortation: "Do nothing from selfishness or empty conceit, but with humility of mind let each of you regard one another as more important than himself (Phil. 2:3). Humility! That is the key to harmony. True humility is expressed by laying aside our own rights and interests and submitting to others. "Do not merely look out for your own personal interests, but also for the interests of others" (v. 4). In other words, have the mind of Christ (v. 5), for that is exactly what He did.

In the description that follows, the predominant characteristic of our Saviour is His humility. "Who, although He existed in the form of God, did not regard equality with God a thing to be grasped" (v. 6). Jesus Christ existed long before He acquired a body in the womb of Mary. He is the eternal Son of God. His existence "in the form of God" has no reference to His outward appearance, for God has no form in that sense of the term. It refers to His essential attributes and inner nature. He possessed divine glory, divine power, and divine authority equal to the Father's. But He did not consider it something to be selfishly held onto at all cost.

Instead, He emptied Himself (v. 7), not of His deity, for He never ceased to be God when He became Man, but of the visible expression of His divine glory and the independent exercise of His divine attributes. His glory was veiled and His attributes were subjected to the will of His Father. In other words, He relinquished the rights of deity which were properly His from all eternity. That was true humility. But the end was not yet.

He took "the form of a bond-servant" (v. 7). A servant has no will of his own. He submits all of his rights to the will of his master. Even so, when Christ came to earth, He not only gave up His divine rights, He gave up *all* His rights. He accepted the status of a slave—subjection, servitude, lowliness, insignificance, and unattractiveness. He lived in poverty and obscurity, and carried out menial tasks. The disciples saw the epitome of His servant's heart the night He took a basin of water and washed their feet.

But here is the most colossal step down: He was "made in the likeness of men" (v. 7). The Creator enters His own creation as a creature—a Man, true Man, with all the limitations of humanity. God became a Man. Again, the emphasis is on humility. "And being found in appearance as a Man, He humbled Himself by becoming obedient to the point of death, even death on a cross" (v. 8)—the lowest, most shameful form of death in the world of His day. God the Son, Possessor and Dispenser of eternal life, agreed to die. But note well, He was *obedient* unto death. Other men die of necessity. He died in willing obedience, another indication of His humble submission to His Father's will.

Crucifixion was reserved for the dregs of society—non-Roman slaves, criminals, murderers, and insurrectionists. Roman citizens were protected by law from death by crucifixion. It was so shameful that the Old Testament placed a curse on anyone who died in that manner (Gal. 3:13; cf. Deut. 21:23). And Christ voluntarily submitted to that curse in order to secure our eternal salvation. He had our interests at heart. That is a humble mind.

"Let this mind be in you, which was also in Christ Jesus" (Phil. 2:5, KJV). The mind of Christ is a mind of humility. The word *humility* in Philippians 2:3 is rendered quite literally in the King James Version as "lowliness of mind." Humility is accurately a low mind. Please do not confuse this with a low self-image, someone saying something like, "I'm no good. I can't do anything right. I just make people around me miserable. Besides that, I'm ugly. How could anybody love a person as ugly as me?" That is not humility, but rather a disguised form of selfishness and pride. When we cannot be what we want to be, do what we want to do, act like we want to act, or look like we want to look, we may get resentful and direct our anger against ourselves, getting a perverted satisfaction out of putting ourselves down. That is proud, self-centered rebellion against the God who made us; it is not humility.

True humility is honestly acknowledging who and what we are and accepting it with thankfulness to God. Humility is happily admitting that we are totally dependent on Him for everything, willingly submitting our wills to His authority, and gratefully acknowledging that what He does is best, even if He exalts others above us. In other words, humility is taking our proper place before God. It weeds out self-centeredness, self-exaltation, self-will, self-sufficiency, self-confidence, self-righteousness, and self-glory. It lives to serve God and others. It allows us to give up our own rights and submit to others.

That is not the way of the natural mind. By nature, we clutch what is ours, protect it at all costs, and stand up for our rights. "If we don't, nobody else will," is the rationalization we use. We scratch and claw for everything we think we deserve. We struggle to be first. We serve ourselves rather than others. We boast of our abilities and glory in our achievements. And the world keeps cheering us on, telling us that this is the only way to get ahead. But these actions are totally contrary to the mind of Christ. He said, "The greatest among you will be your servant. For whoever exalts himself will be humbled, and whoever humbles himself will be exalted" (Matt. 23:11-12, NIV).

During a time of economic depression, a baker sent for 20 of the poorest children in town. He pointed to a basket full of loaves of bread. Each child was to help himself to one, and to come back every day at the same time for another loaf until the economic situation improved. The children began to push and shove, searching through the basket for the biggest loaves. They ran off without even a word of thanks. One little girl waited until all the others had finished, picked up the small loaf that was left, thanked the old man kindly, and went home.

The next day the exact same scene was repeated. But when the little girl's mother cut into the loaf that day, she found a pile of shiny silver coins inside. She sent her daughter back to the baker with the money. "No, my child, it was not a mistake," he said. "I had the coins put into the smallest loaf to reward you." This is how the Lord is going to deal with us someday. "Let this mind be in you, which was also in Christ Jesus," a mind of humility.

4
A Mind
to Suffer

How would you like to be holy, to have the inner assurance that your life is pleasing to God, that you are living as you ought to live, doing what you ought to do, and experiencing daily victory over sin? And how would you like to be enjoying the benefits of holiness, such as a liberating freedom from guilt, a deeply satisfying relationship with God, fearless access into His presence, answered prayer, joyful living, fruitful service, and the wonderful expectation of great reward in heaven? I think most Christians would like to have all of that. But when they find out *how* God wants to make them holy and give them these blessings, they slam on their mental brakes and say, "No thanks, Lord. I don't think I want to travel that road."

Do you know God's major method for making us holy? It is by suffering! Unfortunately, that concept is totally foreign to many Christians. They have the mistaken notion that their salvation is supposed to be a heavenly tranquilizer that keeps them perpetually happy by shielding them against everything painful, disagreeable, or upsetting. It comes as a shock for them to learn that God's primary goal for their lives is not so much to make them happy as it is to make them holy; since holiness is the only thing that can produce genuine and lasting happiness. And holiness comes primarily through suffering. That principle is stated in a verse that tells us something further about the mind of Christ.

The Example of Suffering

"Forasmuch then as Christ has suffered for us in the flesh, arm yourselves likewise with the same mind; for he that has suffered in the flesh has ceased from sin" (1 Peter 4:1, KJV). Peter talked quite a bit, in his first epistle, about Christ's sufferings (cf. 2:21-25; 3:18). He emphasized the *injustice* of those sufferings. They were totally undeserved. Christ did no wrong; there was no deceit in His mouth; He suffered for *our* sins rather than His own. He was a just Person suffering for unjust people; yet He never answered back or retaliated in any way. And in that, we are to follow His example. Much has been made in Christendom about following in Christ's steps (1 Peter 2:21); but the whole point of that exhortation, in its context, is a willingness to suffer unjustly. And to reinforce that point, Peter now says that we are to arm ourselves with the same mind Jesus had—a willingness to suffer without any just cause.

To arm yourself was a military expression meaning to take up the proper tools or weapons for warfare. And notice what weapon we need for the spiritual battle in which we are engaged. It is the mind of Christ, a mind to suffer. He is not speaking of a morbid desire to suffer, but rather of a *willingness* to suffer if that is what God allows to come into our lives. The particular word for *mind* that Peter uses here means thought, idea, insight, intent, or purpose. A mind to suffer is not only a willingness to suffer, but also a dedicated resolve or purpose to accept suffering patiently even if it is undeserved. That is the kind of mind-set Jesus had, and He is our example.

It seems as though one of the unstated goals which many Christians have in life is to avoid suffering. We may never admit it, not even to ourselves, but the avoidance of suffering may be one of the basic motivating forces that governs our behavior and shapes our lives. Nobody in his right mind enjoys suffering, and few of us would ever admit that we deserve it. So naturally, if we do not like suffering and we have not done anything to warrant it, we will probably try to avoid it at all cost.

It is hard for some of us to believe that a loving God would even allow us to suffer. We may become quite indignant with Him for permitting us to suffer, and some have even used their sufferings as an excuse to turn their backs on Him. "What right have You to make me suffer like this, God? What have I ever done to deserve it? If that's the way You want to be, I think I'll just go my own way and live my life the way I please."

Basically, many of us live with an anti-suffering mind-set. And that needs to be changed, said Peter. We need to arm ourselves with the same mind Jesus had, a mind to suffer, a willingness to accept trials patiently as part of God's perfect plan for our lives. We need to accept trials without chafing under them, without getting angry with God over them, and without striking back at the people who cause them, even if they are undeserved.

The people to whom Peter wrote this letter were no different from us. They could not believe that God would allow them to suffer either. Peter had to say to them, "Dear friends, do not be surprised at the painful trial you are suffering, as though something strange were happening to you" (1 Peter 4:12, NIV). It should not surprise us that God allows us to suffer. Jesus Himself warned us that it would come. "If the world hates you, keep in mind that it hated Me first. If you belonged to the world, it would love you as its own. As it is, you do not belong to the world, but I have chosen you out of the world. That is why the world hates you. Remember the words I spoke to you: 'No servant is greater than his master.' If they persecuted Me, they will persecute you also. If they obeyed My teaching, they will obey yours also. They will treat you this way because of My name, for they do not know the One who sent Me" (John 15:18-21, NIV).

That is difficult for us to accept. We want to be liked by everybody. Our whole culture is geared to the promotion of that desire, and the advertising industry offers us one product after another to make us more attractive, better smelling, more appealing, and more popular. But we cannot always be popular. We are not very popular with Satan, and there is no reason to believe we will be popular with Satan's people. Jesus told us the same kind of people who rejected Him will reject us.

It is not that God wants us to develop an attitude of Christian masochism that invites opposition by tactlessness and rudeness, pride and superiority, or by personal idiosyncrasies of various kinds. He just wants us to be like Jesus. And if we are, some of the people in the world will hate us, just as they would have hated Him. Remember, however, that the Christlike traits that arouse hatred in some people will attract others, and we will certainly not lack friends. While Jesus stirred up the animosity of Satan's followers, He probably had more friends than anybody else in Israel in His day. But other people still despised Him, and they cried out for His death without any just cause. Some will likewise detest us and possibly even want to destroy us.

While the main thrust of Peter's letter concerned unjust suffering at the hands of unbelievers, the principles he taught relate to any kind of suffering. Life is filled with agony and anguish, such as the loss of a precious loved one, a crippling accident, a layoff at work, a major financial reversal, a terminal illness, or the suffering from excruciating pain. Those same principles will also help us with the minor annoyances of life, for example, the car that won't start when we have an important appointment, or the washing machine we've paid to have fixed three times that still won't work!

The list of life's trials is unending. And we cannot understand why God allows these irritating and exasperating hardships. But why shouldn't He? He let His Son suffer, didn't He? Jesus Christ suffered to a far greater degree than we can ever begin to imagine. And if we believe in a sovereign God who loves us and who controls every circumstance in our lives, we can accept every new crisis in our lives as part of God's blueprint to make us holy and with an attitude of thanksgiving.

The Benefit of Suffering

Look at the verse again. "Forasmuch then as Christ has suffered for us in the flesh, arm yourselves likewise with the same mind: for he that has suffered in the flesh has ceased from sin" (1 Peter 4:1, KJV). There it is, plainly stated—suffering is part of God's strategy to give us victory over sin and to help us live according to His will. To cease from sin does not imply that we will never do anything wrong after we have suffered, but that suffering will help release us from the power and domination of sin over our lives. Suffering helps deliver us from our enslavement to sin. It becomes a mighty motivation to obey God.

In Scripture, suffering is closely linked to obedience, even in the experience of the Lord Jesus. He had no sin from which He needed to be released, but the writer to the Hebrews does tell us some unusual things about the benefits of suffering in Jesus' life. For example, we read that it pleased the Father to make the Author of our salvation perfect through suffering (Heb. 2:10). The word *perfect* means essentially "complete." Jesus was never less than morally perfect, but there was a sense in which suffering completed His life. It provided what was necessary to demonstrate that He was perfectly submissive to His Father's will and therefore qualified to offer Himself in our place, and to assure us that He was and is a sympathetic and compassionate High Priest who can identify with our needs. Suffering was necessary to equip Him fully and completely to be our Saviour. It was an essential part of His life. He needed to suffer.

Again, the writer to the Hebrews said, "Although He was a Son, He learned obedience from the things which He suffered" (Heb. 5:8). There never was a time when Jesus Christ was disobedient to His Father's will. He was born with the disposition to obey. Yet He learned to obey in actual practice through suffering. Suffering helped Him understand experientially what obedience entails. For example, as He agonized in the garden, facing the weight of the world's sins and the horror of separation from His Father, offering up prayers with loud crying and tears (Heb. 5:7), and sweating great drops of blood (Luke 22:44), He reaffirmed as the steadfast objective of His life complete obedience to His Father's wishes. "Not My will, but Thine be done," He cried (Luke 22:42) with a new comprehension of what obedience really was. He needed to suffer to learn obedience.

Now if Jesus Christ needed to suffer, how much more do we? We have no natural inclination to obey. Our bent is to disobey; so for us, suffering is a discipline that teaches us *to be obedient*. The writer to the Hebrews helps us once more: "No discipline seems pleasant at the time, but painful. Later on, however, it produces a harvest of righteousness and peace for those who have been trained by it" (Heb. 12:11, NIV). He is telling us that the discipline of suffering results in a life of righteousness.

That is exactly what Peter said. The power of sin is often broken in the life of a believer who has experienced deep trials. Somehow those trials tend to give him a new perspective on life, a new set of values, new priorities and goals. Things that once seemed so important now matter very little, and things that were once of secondary importance take on new significance. As Peter put it, because of that suffering, he "does not live the rest of his earthly life for evil human desires, but rather for the will of God" (1 Peter 4:2, NIV).

How does that work? What is it about suffering that aids the development of righteousness, holiness, and godliness, that helps give us victory over sin and a heightened desire to do God's will? In some cases our suffering is the direct result of our sin. In those instances, we learn how unpleasant the consequences of our sin can be, and desiring to avoid unpleasantness, we decide to obey. We have learned obedience through suffering.

But what about the suffering Peter was talking about— suffering that is not caused by sin, suffering that may even be provoked by a courageous stand for righteousness—like the business executive who loses his job because he will not participate in booze parties with his bosses, or the sales manager who gets demoted because he will not misrepresent his product, or the wife whose unsaved husband rails at her because she insists on forgiving a neighbor who treats them badly? And what about the suffering that seems to have no sensible reason to it whatsoever—like the gifted son whose life is snuffed out in an automobile accident, or the devastating fire that wipes out every earthly possession? How can things like that make us holy?

For one thing, they grab hold of our attention and make us alert to what God wants to do in our lives. We may be rocking along rather contentedly in our spiritual life, getting a little careless in our personal relationship with Christ, not giving much heed to what God wants to say to us or accomplish in us. It is easy to get into a rut, to become satisfied with our spiritual progress and insensitive to the things God wants to change. But when tragedy strikes, suddenly we are awake and alert, listening with a keen spiritual ear, ready to look at those areas of our lives to which we were previously blinded, ready to acknowledge responsibilities which we had previously overlooked.

The Apostle Paul had that experience. God had been gracious to him, had blessed his life, had used him effectively to bring blessing to the lives of others, and had revealed to him great spiritual truths. As a result, there was a temptation and possibly even a tendency to be proud which Paul evidently did not recognize. Then God allowed him to experience physical suffering, "a thorn in the flesh." Here is how Paul explained it: "And because of the surpassing greatness of the revelations, for this reason, to keep me from exalting myself, there was given me a thorn in the flesh, a messenger of Satan to buffet me—to keep me from exalting myself!" (2 Cor. 12:7) God had Paul's attention through that thorn, and He was saying, "Paul, I don't want you to get puffed up over these things." Paul had no doubt about what God wanted to do in his life. God had taught him and directed him through suffering.

One young couple I know prayed diligently for something

to bring them out of their spiritual lethargy. It was not long before the doctors detected a tumor on the husband's brain. Their subsequent experience with God has been anything but lethargic. Not only have they come to know Him with new reality, but they have discovered some other things God has wanted to deal with in their lives. Suffering may be compared to a bit in a horse's mouth. It gets our attention, makes us alert, and keeps us moving in the right direction.

For another thing, suffering reminds us of our weaknesses and makes us more consciously dependent on God's power. When things are running smoothly and everything is going our way, we have a tendency to become self-sufficient. We begin to think we can handle any situation ourselves, and so we slip into the habit of operating in the energy of the flesh rather than in conscious dependence on the Lord. There is nothing like a crisis to jolt us back to reality. Suddenly, we become aware of our limitations, our weaknesses, and our utter vulnerability.

That was what happened to Paul in his suffering. He became conscious of his need for divine strength, and the Lord was right there to provide it: "My grace is sufficient for you, for My power is made perfect in weakness" (2 Cor. 12:9, NIV). And when we are operating in Christ's power rather than in our own, we are growing in holiness.

Suffering likewise gives God an opportunity to make Himself known to us with greater reality and intimacy. We often lose the awareness of His presence when everything is sailing along smoothly. But when suffering comes, we turn around and discover that God is right there where He always was, caring, comforting, loving, guiding, directing, providing, and protecting. We get to know Him better. And nothing will promote holy living more effectively than a thorough personal acquaintance with the Holy One Himself.

The benefits of suffering in the life of a believer are immense, and the potential for spiritual growth through suffering is unlimited. But why doesn't suffering always produce these results? Why don't some Christians grow through suffering? Why do some seem to lose ground spiritually, and others even turn their backs on God?

The Danger of Suffering

Unfortunately, not everybody wants to learn obedience, and not everybody wants to live his life in submission to God's will. Holiness is out of style in most quarters today. Submission to authority is contrary to the spirit of our age. The "in" philosophy is resistance to authority, and it pervades nearly every avenue of life. Wives are encouraged to repudiate their husbands' authority. Children are encouraged to disregard their parents' authority. Employees are encouraged to buck their employers' authority. Citizens are encouraged to disobey their government's authority when the laws are not to their liking. With that kind of influence on our thinking, it becomes increasingly difficult for us to bow before the authority of God. We do not want to submit to His will. So why should we willingly accept suffering (something we do not like) when its purpose is to help us submit to God (something we do not want to do)?

That is why I began this chapter by asking, "Would you like to be holy?" If you do not see the tremendous advantages of holiness both in this life and in preparation for the life to come, you will not have a mind to suffer. Suffering will only make you angry and resentful; you will blame God and strike out at other people. You will despise it (Heb. 12:5). You will refuse to be "trained" by it (Heb. 12:11). And instead of yielding the peaceable fruit of righteousness, suffering will cause a root of bitterness to spring up and trouble you (Heb. 12:15).

That danger always exists when God allows suffering to enter our lives. Suffering seldom leaves us as it finds us. It either draws us closer to God and inspires holy living, or it drives a wedge between us and leaves us cold, hard, and bitter. But the choice is ours to make. We cannot blame God for what happens. He is bound by His own holy nature to make available to us opportunities for growth in holiness, and He does so in spite of the dangers. If we sincerely want to grow, we will have a mind like Christ's, a mind to suffer.

5
A Mind
to Grow

Where are the Christians who have the mind of Christ, and who are able to read the Scriptures, understand what God is saying, and then bring their thoughts and ideas into harmony with His? Some people who claim to be Christians have already made up their minds about what they believe and how they are going to live. When they hear some new truth presented from God's Word that should affect the way they live, their reaction is to question it, to find some way to protect themselves against it, and to look for some good reason to reject it. Because they have formed a habit pattern of turning their minds off to the truth of God's Word, they are largely unfamiliar with the content of the Bible and uncomfortable talking about spiritual things. When the conversation moves beyond the simplest tenets of the Christian faith, they are utterly at a loss to make any contribution. And they seem perfectly content to remain that way.

There were some folks at Corinth like that. So after discussing the ability of a spiritual person to comprehend the deep things of God, Paul turned to those folks and said by way of contrast, "And I, brethren, could not speak to you as to spiritual men, but as to men of flesh, as to babes in Christ. I gave you milk to drink, not solid food; for you were not yet able to receive it. Indeed, even now you are not yet able" (1 Cor. 3:1-2). They could not understand much of the Scriptures. They were still on the milk bottle as far as their ability to receive spiritual truth was concerned. They were spiritual babies.

There is nothing wrong with a baby. We were all babies at one point in our lives, and most of us have later had some babies of our own to enjoy. They are a source of great wonder and delight. But a baby turns from being a source of joy to a source of concern when he does not grow. We try to find out what is wrong with him and then do something about it. The same is true in the spiritual realm. Those spiritual babies at Corinth were a source of concern to Paul. He expected them to grow because that is what normal, healthy, living beings do. Their lack of growth was a tragedy, and something had to be done to correct it.

One thing is quite clear about growth, however—it does not come through personal effort. A lily does not grow by toiling (Matt. 6:28), and we do not grow by stretching. At five feet eight inches tall, I would certainly add a few inches to my height if I could do it by trying. But Jesus assures me that no amount of anxious struggling will contribute to my growth (Matt. 6:27). Growth is the result of the life principle within; so spiritual growth will not come through self-effort. We are not going to develop into spiritual adults who have the mind of Christ by struggling to imitate Him in the power of our human wills or in the energy of our flesh. Our growth will come as the natural expression of Christ's life within us. Apart from that life flowing from the vine to the branches, there can be neither growth nor fruit (John 15:4).

And yet there is something we must do. The Apostle Peter issued a command to us when he said, "But grow in the grace and knowledge of our Lord and Saviour Jesus Christ" (2 Peter 3:18). The very fact that he used an imperative demonstrates that this is something for which we are responsible; this is something we must do. We decide whether or not we are going to grow.

This is such a confusing thing to so many Christians. On one hand, it looks as though there is nothing we can do. On the other hand, it looks as though we are expected to do something. It seems as if every speaker on the subject of spiritual growth and victorious Christian living has a little different emphasis. One tells us we must confess our sins and appropriate the filling of the Spirit by faith; so we try that for awhile. Someone else says we need to reckon ourselves to be dead to sin and then live the crucified life; so we endeavor to practice that for awhile. Then a third comes along and insists that we need to put forth every effort like a runner reaching for the goal; so we give that a try—until we hear someone else say that we need to stop striving in the energy of the flesh and rest in Christ's power. And the average Christian is totally bewildered.

Who is right? Actually they are *all* right. Every one of those concepts is biblical and each one plays a part in our spiritual growth. But we must get started somewhere. We must begin to put each of those principles into practice, and that depends ultimately on having a mind to grow.

Paul penned a crucial passage to the Philippians on the subject of spiritual growth, and he related it unmistakably to the mind. "Let us therefore, as many as be perfect, be thus minded," he said (Phil. 3:15, KJV). To be *perfect* is to be mature or growing. Growing Christians think in a certain way; they have a certain kind of mind-set. To understand what kind that is, we need to go back and see what Paul was talking about in this chapter.

He shared with his readers the goals of his life: to know Christ intimately, thoroughly, and experientially, to demonstrate the power of His resurrection in everyday living, and to realize the precious fellowship with Him that comes through God-appointed suffering. Paul wanted to demonstrate in his daily walk what it meant to be identified with Christ in His death and resurrection (Phil. 3:10-11). In other words, he wanted to be like Jesus. Was he there yet? Certainly not! And he frankly admitted it.

An Honest Mind

"Not that I have already obtained it, or have already become perfect" (Phil. 3:12). The word *perfect* here is slightly different from the one used in verse 15. This one means to bring to completion. Paul was saying, "I haven't arrived yet; I haven't reached a state of absolute completion; I haven't attained my final goal of Christlikeness. God isn't finished with me yet." And just to be sure we understand it, he said it again: "Brethren, I do not regard myself as having laid hold of it yet" (Phil. 3:13). In other words, "I still do not possess as my own all the Christlike characteristics that I should have. I haven't laid hold of everything I ought to be. I don't know Christ as well as I should know Him. I haven't experienced all the resurrection power I can experience. I am not yet perfect!"

Do you know why Paul said that? Because some professing Christians at Philippi were claiming it was possible to reach complete sanctification in this life, a state of perfection in which any further growth was unnecessary. And that is a dangerous doctrine! It breeds spiritual sterility, self-righteousness, and pride. And that leads to contention and strife. If you put two people together who both think they are perfect, you have the makings of a good fight. You see, if they disagree on anything, neither one of them will give in. They will both believe they are right. So they will have to stand up for their opinions, defend themselves, and prove the other person wrong; and they may even get a little heated up when they do it. The ludicrous result will be two people who say they can do no wrong, but are doing wrong and are exhibiting all the fleshliness they say they do not have.

But here was one of the greatest and godliest men who ever lived, honestly admitting that he had not arrived. Isn't it rather ridiculous for us to claim that we need no more growth when the Apostle Paul admitted that he still needed to grow? I think most of us really know better. We may even let the crack in our armor show once in awhile, as when a stubborn husband or wife admits in a weak moment, "I know I'm not perfect, but . . . " and then goes on to point out his mate's faults, which are in his eyes the real source of the problem. Unfortunately he still will not admit anything specific, because then he will be obligated before God to change it. He is often unwilling to go to anyone for help, for then his weaknesses will be brought to light, and, again, he will have to change. He will rather insist, "There's nothing wrong with me. If there's a problem between us, it's your problem, not mine. I've grown all I need to grow. I've given all I'm going to give. You can go for help if you want, but I don't need it."

I was good at this in the early years of our marriage. We had a very difficult time adjusting. Mary admits that she started the trouble most of the time, and that was the best reason in the world for me not to admit my faults. Whenever she tried to get me to see them, I would respond with something like, "Look, I never said I was perfect." But I wasn't about to admit what my imperfections were. I am not sure I even knew what they were. And it was too threatening for me to try to find out. There was little hope of our marriage growing until we were both willing to be honest. The Apostle Paul had an honest mind, and he reminded us that if we are as grown-up as we think we are, we will develop honest minds too. If we refuse, Paul is confident that God will show us the fallacy of our self-righteous attitude in some way or other (Phil. 3:15).

A Highly-Motivated Mind

But honestly admitting our imperfections is not going to solve anything in and of itself. Some people are finally forced to admit that they are not perfect, and it almost destroys them. They go from one extreme to another: "I'm no good, I never will be. I don't know how anybody can even stand me. There's no sense in going on." That is a clever ploy to gain sympathy and get people to tell us that we're not so bad after all. And that's what we really thought all along. God wants us to stop playing those kinds of games and do something about our imperfections. That's what Paul did.

"But I press on in order that I may lay hold of that for which also I was laid hold of by Christ Jesus" (Phil. 3:12). *I press on* is a racing term Paul borrowed from the stadium. It means to follow after or to pursue, and it pictures a runner straining every muscle as he heads down the final stretch. It is the eager pursuit of a definite goal. Paul may not have been perfect, but he was not going to sit around crying about it, feeling sorry for himself, and making the same mistakes over and over again. He was going to press on toward a specific goal. By God's grace, he was going to become the man whom God envisioned when He stopped Paul in his tracks on the Damascus Road and saved him. Paul was going to take hold of that for which Christ took hold of him. And he was going to go at it with all the diligence and discipline of a track star going after the coveted gold medal. Then, after admitting the second time that he had not yet arrived, he added, "But this one thing I do" (Phil. 3:13, KJV). He had singleness of purpose. He was goal oriented, and was going to apply himself wholeheartedly to reaching his goal.

After that expression of his determined purpose, Paul was ready to give us his strategy for running the Christian race. Here was how he intended to grow into the man of God he knew he ought to be: "But one thing I do; forgetting what lies behind and reaching forward to what lies ahead, I press on toward the goal for the prize of the upward call of God in Christ Jesus" (Phil. 3:13-14). Here then was his threefold strategy for growth.

First, forget the past. There is no way that we can grow into the likeness of Christ by living in the past. While we cannot obliterate it from our minds, we do not need to fix our attention on it. Living in the past, whether it is good or bad, is like tying a noose around our spiritual growth. For example, letting our minds dwell on what we were before we met Christ can paralyze us with discouragement. Focusing our minds on the failures we have experienced since our salvation will lead to more failures now. And while the victories of the past hold pleasant memories that we can rightfully enjoy, letting them monopolize our thoughts can swell us with pride or lull us into self-satisfaction, complacency, and indifference. Living on yesterday's spiritual mountain-top experiences will keep us from scaling new spiritual heights today. Insisting on doing things as we have always done them in the past may cause us to miss God's methods for the present. We can learn from the past, but what's done is done. We must consciously put the past out of our minds by an act of our wills and forget it!

Second, reach for what lies ahead. This is another racing term that means, literally, "to stretch forward." The runners are approaching the finish line now. They are using every ounce of energy they can muster. Their bodies are bent forward, stretching for the tape. The race may be decided by a fraction of an inch, and the one who stretches the most will be crowned the victor. That was the kind of desire Paul had to grow in Christ. That was the kind of diligence he poured into it. His strategy for growth was to make it the one great passion of his life.

Do we share Paul's dedicated purpose, or are we satisfied to coast along much like we are? "I'm at least as good as the average Christian, so why should I get all excited about growing?" Here is why we should grow—for the glory of God who saved us, for the fullest effectiveness and joy in our Christian lives right here and now, and for the reward we shall receive at the judgment seat of Christ. And that reward was the thing in Paul's mind when he gave us the next element of his strategy.

Third, press toward the goal. "I press on toward the goal for the prize of the upward call of God in Christ Jesus" (Phil. 3:14). That high calling (or upward call), in this context, is to be like Jesus. And for those who pursue it with steadfast endurance, there is a prize, a reward. Paul pursued it. It was the central, controlling force in his life. He was motivated by the highest and noblest ideals of which a human being is capable, the desire to grow into the likeness of Jesus Christ. And he said that if we are as mature as we think we are, we will have the same highly motivated mind to grow. We will not only forget the past, and reach for what lies ahead; we will press toward the goal of Christlikeness.

Maybe we should ask ourselves a few questions before we go on. "Are we more like Christ than we used to be? Are we growing into His likeness? Are we able to look into His Word, see the changes He wants to make in us, then move ahead by faith to let Him make them?" We know that we cannot make any of those changes in our own strength. These changes have to be the results of His work in us. But we will never even get started until we make up our minds to grow.

There are many factors involved in spiritual growth. We must reprogram our thought patterns with God's Word, then step out by faith and obey Him. We must press on to Christlikeness with the zeal of a runner on the home stretch. We must do it, not in the energy of the flesh, but in total dependence on Christ's power. We must confess our sins and appropriate the filling of the Spirit by faith. We must consider ourselves to be dead to sin and alive to God. We must yield our bodies as instruments of righteousness to God. All of these things are important, but they all begin in the mind. We act in accord with the thoughts in our minds; so we cannot do what God wants us to until we think as God wants us to think. Technically, we are free to choose any course of action, but we will not act contrary to the information in our minds. If we want to grow, we will need to cultivate a mind to grow.

6
The Mind Screen

We have learned that one part of God's strategy for our spiritual growth is for us to forget the past, but that is easier said than done. More than once I have talked with an earnest seeker who desired to grow, but who with anxiety on his face and anguish in his voice has pleaded, "Please tell me how I can stop thinking about my sinful past."

There is no easy solution to that problem, but there are some helpful suggestions. For one thing, we can learn to alert ourselves to destructive thoughts. One way would be to devise some sort of startling signal to use on ourselves as soon as we realize that we are reflecting on past sins or other harmful thoughts. Some folks speak right out loud and say, "Stop!" in order to jar themselves back to reality. For them that is a reminder to turn off those injurious ponderings and put their minds back into gear for more profitable things. Once we alert ourselves to what we are doing, then by an act of our wills, through the power of the Holy Spirit, we can eliminate those injurious mental meanderings and learn to control our thoughts.

But we all know from experience that we will not keep those damaging thoughts away very long unless we replace them with wholesome thoughts. Just as air rushes to fill a vacuum, so unwholesome thoughts rush back into an empty mind. What we need is a grid to screen what we let settle down in our minds and become part of our lives—a measuring rod or testing device to examine and filter our thoughts. If we could evaluate every thought by such a standard, then discard those that do not measure up and accept only those that make a profitable contribution to our lives, we would be able to keep our minds free of what is damaging and detrimental. Thus, we would enjoy mental health and happiness as well as spiritual growth.

Did you know that God has provided us with just such a mind screen? It is revealed in one penetrating verse of Scripture: "Finally, brethren, whatever is true, whatever is honorable, whatever is right, whatever is pure, whatever is lovely, whatever is of good repute, if there is any excellence and if anything worthy of praise, let your mind dwell on these things" (Phil. 4:8).

There is one finite verb in that verse and it is a command. Let your mind *dwell* on these things. In other words, *think!* Some folks don't like that. They did not know that the Christian life required them to use their brain cells. They would be more comfortable if Paul had said, "Feel!" But he wanted us to use our heads. And the word he chose means more than merely to keep something in our minds. *Dwell* means to consider, ponder, and reflect; to mull it over and meditate on it. It involves focusing our attention on something, letting our minds linger on it. The verb occurs in the present tense, which emphasizes continuous action. We are to keep on focusing our attention on these things, continuously.

If the Holy Spirit of God tells us to fix our attention on certain things, we must be able to do it. God made us with volition, and we can choose what we think about. Fleeting thoughts may invade our minds periodically, but God has given us the ability to cast them aside—to or let them linger. That is our decision to make. If we make the right decision, and then replace the unwholesome thoughts with those that fit into God's eightfold grid, we will be able to protect our minds from the thoughts that keep us spiritually static and stunted. Here then are eight questions by which we can sift our thoughts.

Is It True?

The word *true* refers not only to what is true in contrast to what is false, but to what is true in the sense of being real or genuine. A Christian should obviously refuse to dwell on things he knows to be false. Dwelling on falsehoods perverts our outlook on life and tangles our lives with complicated problems of our own making. Lies destroy us. They have no place in a healthy Christian mind. Since God is true (John 3:33) and His Word is true (John 17:17), we should think a great deal about Him, and let the concepts of His Word dominate our minds.

But there is that further idea of being real or genuine. Too many Christians seek to escape reality. They don't want to admit the real problems in their lives. They avoid coming to grips with their limitations, weaknesses, and sins. They seem to think that if they close their eyes to the truth, it will go away; so they devise clever ways to keep from facing the facts. Some escape to the world of make-believe. They spend excessive amounts of time watching television or reading unwholesome novels. They identify with soap opera heroes and heroines; they fill their minds with fantasy and illusion, and then wonder why they cannot cope with the real problems of real life.

One Christian woman acknowledged to me how much more irritably she acted toward her husband when she watched soap operas regularly. Everything in the story was beautiful. While the characters had their problems, the bills were always paid; the women never had to cook, do housework, or care for the children; and the problems themselves somehow seemed glamorous and inviting. She found herself envying the people in the stories, resenting her own responsibilities, and taking this resentment out on her husband. She had violated the first principle of God's mind screen:

"Is it real?"

This is not to imply that a Christian can never enjoy fiction of any kind. Jesus told fictional stories to illustrate truth. But there was spiritual reality in what He said. When we fill our minds with the hollow and illusive philosophy of Satan's world system, we are sowing the seeds of future mental distress.

Is It Honorable?

The word *honorable* refers to what is worthy of honor or inspires respect. It actually comes from a word that relates to worship, and refers to being dignified, noble, serious, or valuable. It is the opposite of flippant and frivolous. Paul is not implying that Christians can never have fun. Christians can have more real fun than non-Christians because their fun is not a desperate attempt to compensate for a gnawing emptiness or loneliness. Christians don't become frustrated and depressed when the party is over. Having fun is part of the fullness of life they experience in Christ.

But the healthy mind is not always occupied with foolishness and nonsense, with fun and games. It is a mind that has seriousness of purpose and self-respect in conduct. As such, it inspires respect from others. One reason some of us are experiencing mental turmoil is our belief that nobody respects us. Respect can be earned, not by demanding it, but by occupying our minds with things of real significance and value, things such as knowing and doing the will of God. That will soon become evident to others around us and it will inspire their respect. What do we think about most of the time? Are these thoughts about things of honest value?

Is It Right?

The word *right* means upright, righteous, and conforming to the principles of God's Word. It refers to the right way of looking at things, that is, looking at things from God's perspective. Paul used this same word earlier in his letter to the Philippians. He told them he was confident that God would continue to perform the good work He had begun in them;

then he said, "For it is only right for me to feel this way about you all" (Phil. 1:7). It was right in that it was consistent with the character of God as revealed in the Word. When thoughts came into Paul's mind, he evaluated them from God's viewpoint, according to the standard of His Word. If his thoughts were right he embraced them; if they were wrong he rejected them.

Every day Satan seeks to feed his false philosophy into our minds through the media, through unbelieving friends, relatives, teachers, and fellow workers. But God wants us to develop the habit of asking, "Is that right? Is it consistent with God's Word?" We need to identify Satan's lies for what they are, then reject them.

If we use this grid when we watch television, we may decide to quit watching it altogether. There are very few programs in which we cannot identify something contrary to the Scripture. In a few weeks of soap opera watching, someone cataloged the following list of occurrences: wife beatings, child abuse, rape, a favorable view of the occult, beautiful extramarital affairs, and easy divorces that never seemed to affect the children adversely. And incidentally, these comments about soap operas are not directed solely to women. One survey revealed that half the viewers are now men, some retired, some out of work, some on welfare, and others merely on their lunch hour. Why do we keep exposing our minds to Satan's propaganda? It only confuses us and keeps us from growing in our walk with God.

Is It Pure?

The word *pure* has reference to moral purity, the absence of anything that stains, defiles, contaminates, or corrupts, particularly in sexual matters. And God labels all premarital and extramarital sex, as well as homosexuality, *impure*. I know some professing Christians who have become slaves to unclean thoughts. Their impure thoughts have led to immoral acts, and the results have been minds that are riddled with guilt and shame, accompanied by feelings of worthlessness and despair which are conducive neither to spiritual growth nor good mental health. That downward spiral invariably began when they willfully chose to let their minds dwell on impure things: lewd literature, music with suggestive lyrics, movies with immoral themes, and television programs that aroused sexual thoughts. There came a time when they could not seem to help themselves any more. They grew to hate their immorality; it brought no real satisfaction to their lives, but they could not escape from its clutches.

If you find yourself in a similar predicament, God has grace available for you right now to forgive and to deliver. But you will need to begin screening every thought from this moment on, and refusing to dwell on those that are impure.

I have talked with parents who are concerned about questionable behavior in the lives of their teenagers. But they have overlooked the incisive truth that we often reap in our children the fruits of our own impurity. When we are careless about what we feed into our minds, our children notice it, and it affects their own moral perspective. We may have nobody to blame but ourselves when our teenagers get into moral difficulties. Before we let our eyes gaze on it, our ears listen to it, or our minds think about it, we need to ask ourselves, "Is it pure?"

Is It Lovely?

The word *lovely* refers to what is attractive, pleasing, winsome, amiable, or agreeable. Even sinful things can be attractive to us, so maybe *amiable* would be the best word to sum up its meaning. This word represents the pleasantness and graciousness that foster peace and harmony. If we are mulling over matters that increase tension and strife with someone, we are not growing in the Lord or enjoying peace of mind. If we keep thinking about a nasty remark somebody made about us, or a dirty trick he played on us, it will keep us tied in knots.

We need to forgive! And every time that disagreeable thought comes back to our minds, we need to ask God to help us forget. Then we should begin thinking about something in that person which inspires love and harmony. We ought to go out of our way to be pleasant and kind. It will do wonders for our mental health as well as for our relationships with the Lord and with others. Test that thought! Is it amiable?

Is It of Good Repute?

The phrase *good repute* comes from a word that means, literally, "to speak well of." In other words, we are to think of the good things in other people, the things that speak well of them, that put them in a good light. If we want to maintain a healthy, happy, growing mind, we should not even listen to things that put others in a bad light. Our old sin nature relishes such information because it makes us feel superior in that we are not like them, as well as knowledgeable in that we have inside information which others do not have. Knowing uncomplimentary things about them also gives us the upper hand, and causes us to get puffed up with self-righteousness and pride. But in the end, it brings nothing but spiritual decline and mental distress. For one thing, it affects our attitude toward the persons in question, which they probably sense, and which in turn causes tension between us and them. And if we think about it long enough, we eventually tell someone else; and that usually gets back to the persons we gossiped about, complicating our problems even more.

Some will protest, "But I thought it was gossip only if it wasn't true." No! It is gossip when it puts someone else in a bad light, whether it is true or false. If we know something derogatory about another believer, God wants us to talk to that person about it before we breathe a word to anyone else (Matt. 18:15; cf. Gal. 6:1). After that, our only reason for telling others would be to solicit their help in restoring the erring Christian, or to protect him from something that would be damaging to his spiritual progress. What a giant step we would take toward harmonious relations with others, toward spiritual growth, and toward mental stability if we would commit ourselves to thinking and talking only about things of good repute!

Is It Excellent?

Paul adds two more traits to his mind screen. He changes the format here and uses nouns instead of adjectives: "If there is any excellence and if anything worthy of praise, let your mind dwell on these things" (Phil. 4:8). The Greek word translated "excellence" is a difficult word to interpret. It is only used four times in the New Testament, the other three being in Peter's epistles (cf. 1 Peter 2:9; 2 Peter 1:3, 5). In the early Greek world, this word meant excellence of achievement or manly courage. During the time of the Maccabees, it referred to the steadfastness of the martyrs unto death. Later it came to be applied to God, His splendor, and His might.

The word seems to refer to that which rises above the mundane, transitory, hollow things of this world, to that which is of moral excellence. It involves things that are associated with God's glory and power, things that have eternal value.

Do you want to have a stable, spiritually vigorous mind? Stop dwelling on second-rate matter, things like material possessions, bank accounts, and status with friends. Much mental distress and spiritual defeat can be directly related to the failure to get the *things* you want in life. If you fix your attention on eternity's values, then live to glorify Christ and to know His resurrection power, you shall escape that satanic pitfall. And that is true excellence.

Is It Praiseworthy?

This could mean, "Does it deserve your praise?" Others say the word *praiseworthy* means, "Does it have the praise of God? Does God look on it with approval?" It does not matter a great deal which view we take, for nothing deserves our praise unless it has God's approval. And that just about sums it all up. Everything else on the list could be included with this one. If we want healthy, happy, spiritually robust minds, we need to ask ourselves this question before letting our minds dwell on anything: "Is this something that God would want me to be thinking about? Does it please Him? Would it bring praise from Him?"

Some folks are going to object to this. "That's too rigid. I can't live that way." We really don't have to. It's our choice to make. But we should know that most mental and emotional disturbances, as well as most debilitating sins, begin by allowing our minds to dwell on things that God would never condone. We can go on suffering spiritual mediocrity and mental distress if we so choose; or we can begin to enjoy spiritual growth and mental stability God's way, by filtering every thought through God's mind screen and allowing only those thoughts that please Him to settle down and remain.

We will enjoy healthy, happy, and spiritually flourishing minds when we think on things that:

- are true and real;
- are worthy of respect;
- are conforming to the principles of God's Word;
- are morally pure;
- foster peace and harmony;
- speak well of other people;
- rise above the mundane; and
- bring praise from God.

There we have it—God's grid to filter our thoughts.

7
A Sound Mind

Mental health is a prominent subject in our day. The government, at various levels, has assumed the responsibility of providing adequate mental-health services and care for its citizens. Clinics are available all over the country to help people develop sound mental health and to help them learn how they can adjust to their environment, with maximum effectiveness and a sense of happiness and well-being.

But it seems that with all the effort being expended and all the money being spent, more people are suffering from mental illness than ever before. Facilities are overcrowded, qualified personnel are overworked, and people sometimes wait for weeks in order to see someone who can help them. It seems to be a losing battle.

Did you know that God is also interested in the subject of mental health? "For God has not given us the spirit of fear; but of power, and of love, and of a sound mind" (2 Tim. 1:7, KJV). The words *sound mind* are the translation of one Greek word which means, literally, "saving the mind." The Greek word refers to a mind that has been salvaged for its intended purpose. While this particular word is used only once in the entire New Testament, related words from the same root are used 16 times. By tracing the various uses of this entire word group, we can learn what God has to say about a sound mind, and how He intends for us to enjoy good mental health.

The first time one of these words is used refers to the demoniac of Gadara. He had been out of his mind, running through cemeteries naked, screaming, cutting himself with stones, and breaking the chains which people had used to bind him. But after Jesus cast the demons out, he was found calmly sitting at Jesus' feet, clothed and "in his right mind" (Mark 5:15; Luke 8:35). There the word obviously means to be sane, sensible, rational, reasonable, and in control of one's mental faculties.

Paul used another of the words in the same way. He was giving his personal testimony to King Agrippa and Governor Festus, and he came to the part about the resurrection of Jesus Christ. "At this point Festus interrupted Paul's defense. 'You are out of your mind, Paul!' he shouted. 'Your great learning is driving you insane.'

'I am not insane, most excellent Festus,' Paul replied. 'What I am saying is true and reasonable'" (Acts 26:24-25, NIV). Paul was not crazy. His words were *reasonable*, that is, sane and rational; he showed good judgment and good sense. And that is the basic idea of a sound mind. It is a mind saved from uselessness, unprofitableness, futility, and worthlessness. It is a mind that shows good judgment and good sense.

Characteristics of Sound-Minded People

Now look at some of the areas of life to which God applies the things that make good sense for a believer. Here are three characteristics of a sound-minded person.

First, *he views himself realistically*. "For through the grace given to me I say to every man among you not to think more highly of himself than he ought to think; but to think so as to have sound judgment, as God has allotted to each a measure of faith" (Rom. 12:3). The Greek word meaning "to have sound judgment" is one of these words that means to be sane, sensible, rational, and reasonable. It occurs in a context about spiritual gifts. When a person overestimates himself, praises himself, is puffed up with his own importance and superiority, or claims to have gifts and abilities which he really does not have, he is not using good judgment. He is actually impairing his mental health.

We can understand that quite readily. If we exaggerate our abilities, and as a result are asked to do things we are really not qualified to do, the consequence will usually be failure, embarrassment, guilt, discouragement, loss of self-esteem, and loss of confidence. In fact, it is possible that the experience could be so traumatic that all further usefulness would be destroyed. That certainly would not do very much for our mental well-being.

The person who wants to maintain a sound mind forms a proper estimate of himself before God. He evaluates his gifts according to the measure of faith God has given him, not according to the desire for prominence, prestige, or power which his old sin nature tries to stir up. And when he exercises his God-given gifts for the glory of God, the results are joy, blessing, the success God intended, and the personal satisfaction of being used by Him. These results contribute to a sound mind. Viewing ourselves realistically makes good sense.

Second, *he keeps his mind clear for prayer.* Peter teaches us this lesson, and it is in a context of suffering. That was a major theme of his first epistle because his readers were experiencing deep trials and were becoming greatly discouraged. But he assured them that there was an end in sight. Jesus was coming again and then all their trials would be over. "The end of all things is at hand; therefore, be of sound judgment and sober spirit for the purpose of prayer" (1 Peter 4:7). "To be of sober spirit" means to have a clear mind, which is not affected by stimulants or depressants. Peter is saying that soundmindedness and sobriety go together. Dulling our senses with drugs or alcohol is poor judgment. It damages sound minds, and people with good sense do not do it.

Most of us need all the help we can get to live the Christian life in these difficult days. The only reliable Source of help is the Lord Himself, and we lay hold of Him through prayer. We are in a battle against a supernatural enemy, and prayer is the key to victory (cf. Eph. 6:12-18). Our prayer lives cannot be very effective when our brains are blunted and our minds are stupefied with intoxicants. It is foolish to do anything that will diminish our ability to approach God's throne of grace intelligently and effectively. It makes good sense to keep our minds clear for prayer.

Third, *he controls his passions and desires.* Paul gets to the root of a sound mind in his letter to Titus. "For the grace of God has appeared, bringing salvation to all men, instructing us to deny ungodliness and worldly desires and to live sensibly, righteously, and godly in the present age" (Titus 2:11-12). Right after encouraging us to repudiate worldly lusts, or control our desires and passions, he encourages us to live sensibly, to be sound minded, and to use good judgment. In other words, sound-mindedness and self-discipline go together. People who want to enjoy a healthy mind must learn to control their passions.

Interestingly, when we study this word group both in secular Greek literature and in the Scriptures, we find that it means not only mental soundness and good judgment, but also self-discipline, self-control, moderation, modesty, and decency. It suggests the total command of our passions and desires.

Some people think that these are strange concepts to put together in one word group. They have the opinion that mental health is enhanced by the lack of restraint and by freedom to do as they please, that restraints are the cause of most neuroses, and that repression leads to mental illness. But it has never worked out that way in actual practice. They may think they need total freedom from all restraint and the privilege of living apart from all personal discipline, but the inevitable result for people who think this way is guilt, depression, and mental turmoil.

That is true in every area of desire and passion. Overeating is an example. You may keep telling yourself that you can eat as much as you want: "It's my body and I can do with it as I please." But the bigger you get, the more guilt you feel, the less you like yourself, and the more depressed you become. So what usually happens is that you eat more to relieve your emotional pain, and that leads to greater mental and emotional distress. Lack of self-control destroys a sound mind.

Suppose you are attracted to a member of the opposite sex to whom you are not married, and that person is attracted to you. You each allow your passions to race unchecked and you end up in bed with each other. You may use every rationalization the world has ever devised, but it does not quench the guilt you feel and the mental anguish you experience. Again, what often happens is that you get more involved physically in an attempt to relieve the emotional pain, and then you feel even more depressed. Lack of self-control destroys a sound mind.

Or maybe your problem is anger. When people cross you or fail to perform to your expectations, you pop your cork and vent your rage. You insist that you have a right to be indignant. But why, then, do you feel so utterly remorseful? Sometimes you alienate your friends by your unruly antics, and that only adds to your mental misery. A lack of personal discipline can never contribute to a sound mind. Proper restraints offer boundaries within which you can operate with freedom and security, leading to confidence and peace of mind. It makes good sense to control your passions and desires.

A Catalog of Sound-Minded People

Now that we have discovered three things involved in a sound mind, we want to deal with the question of who needs to have a sound mind. Who are the people who must view themselves realistically, keep their minds clear for prayer, and control their passions and desires? Who should be sensible and self-controlled?

First, *older men*. Five groups of people are mentioned in the first six verses of Titus 2, a central passage on the subject of the sound mind. The first of these is older men. "Older men are to be temperate, dignified, sensible, sound in faith, in love, in perseverance" (Titus 2:2). That word *sensible* refers to a sound mind, and the *New International Version* renders it "self-controlled." Both ideas are present here and it is difficult to know which one was foremost in Paul's mind. Maybe he felt that both were equally important. He wanted older men to be both sane and sensible on the one hand, and self-disciplined and self-controlled on the other.

If there is one group of people in the local church that needs to set an example in this regard, it is the older men. Their age, their experience, their time studying the Word, and their years of walking with God should have produced a level of godliness, a maturity of judgment, and a degree of personal restraint that challenges and inspires all others.

We have heard a great deal in recent years about "dirty old men" and their off-color antics. Presumably, people laugh at these antics because they think these old men are "just harmless." But God is not laughing! When men who have lived for 65 or 70 years still have not learned that the gratification of physical desires alone can never satisfy the longing of the soul, it is no laughing matter. It is utter insanity. And their actions do immense spiritual damage to others who desperately need worthy models to emulate. The strength of the body of Christ depends heavily on godly older men with sound minds.

Second, *older women*. "Older women likewise are to be reverent in their behavior, not malicious gossips, nor enslaved to much wine, teaching what is good" (Titus 2:3). No word from the word group we are studying actually appears in this verse, but there is no question about the need for older Christian women to be sound minded. For one thing, Paul uses the term "likewise" to link what he is saying with the verse before it. For another, the older women are to teach the younger women to be sound minded, as we shall see shortly. They cannot effectively teach what they have not personally appropriated. And furthermore, the exhortations themselves reveal characteristics of a sound mind: for instance, "not malicious gossips" (they need to control their tongues); or "not enslaved to much wine" (they need to control their appetites). The strength of the body of Christ will also depend on godly older women with sound minds setting a good example for younger women to follow.

Third, *younger women.* I do not know where the line between old women and young women should be drawn, and I am certainly not brave (or foolish) enough to venture a guess. But it does not really matter. Both are to have sound minds. "That they [the older women] may encourage the young women to love their husbands, to love their children, to be sensible, pure, workers at home, kind, being subject to their own husbands, that the Word of God may not be dishonored" (Titus 2:4-5).

There are actually two words from this word group in these two verses. The word translated "encourage" literally means "to cause someone to be sound minded, to bring someone to his senses." No one is better qualified to train young women to be sensible and self-controlled, to be successful wives and mothers, and to be spiritually minded women of God than experienced older women. And one of the things they are to teach young women is to be *sensible.* That is another word from this same word group, and again it is translated "self-controlled" in the *New International Version.* By now we know that "encourage" has both of those ideas—young women are to be sensible and self-controlled.

With regard to young women in particular, this word group takes on an added connotation: the idea found in the King James translation in this verse—"discreet." Paul makes this point more clearly in another epistle. "Likewise, I want women to adorn themselves with proper clothing, modestly and discreetly, not with braided hair and gold or pearls or costly garments" (1 Tim. 2:9). *Discreetly* is the word that relates to the sound mind. God wants Christian women to dress with good sense, good judgment, and self-control.

The Word of God acknowledges that viewing certain parts of the female anatomy arouses temptations in many men that are difficult for them to control. Some women insist that this is the men's problem, not theirs. They feel that women have a right to dress any way they please and men can just look the other way if they have trouble dealing with these temptations. But God's Word places some responsibility on the women. God says a woman who has any sense, who has any self-discipline and self-control, will not dress so as to arouse the desires of the men around her. That is what older Christian women need to teach younger Christian women. That is what Christian mothers need to teach their daughters.

Being a sex object has seldom ever contributed to a woman's mental serenity, stability, or self-worth. Women who have been appreciated for little more than the shapes of their bodies have sometimes decided that their lives are not worth living. It makes good sense to dress modestly. It is part of having a sound mind.

Fourth, *younger men*. The exhortation to young men is brief, but just as important. It says, literally, "Likewise, urge the young men to be sensible" (Titus 2:6). There is no more important issue in the lives of young men who know Christ than to be sensible and self-controlled. The temptations are legion in our materialistic, sex-saturated society. But if young men expect to accomplish anything of significance for the glory of God, or expect to make their lives count for Jesus Christ, then they will need to be sound minded, viewing life from God's perspective and developing Spirit-empowered self-control.

Fifth, *elders*. There are some other people in the local church who need to have sound minds. Of course, everyone has already been included in one way or another, but this group demands special mention; for it is supremely important that elders be sensible and self-controlled. The word translated "sound minded" appears in both lists of qualifications for elders ("prudent," 1 Tim. 3:2; "sensible," Titus 1:8).

Those who rule the church must have mature spiritual judgment, with absolute command over their passions and desires. The work of God on earth is in shambles where it is in the hands of men who lack godly wisdom and Spirit-empowered self-discipline. When an elder goes into a rage or falls into immorality, the damage is sometimes irreparable. We should pray diligently that the leaders of our churches will be men and women of sound minds.

The Provision for Sound-Minded People

Some things in this chapter are difficult for people in our day to accept. The concepts run counter to everything the world is telling us. How is it possible for us to have sound minds when Satan is trying to brainwash us daily? We must go back to 2 Timothy 1:7 again: "For God has not given us the spirit of fear; but of power, and of love, and of a sound mind" (KJV). The provision has already been made. God has given us His Holy Spirit, who energizes our human spirits and gives us the power to be sensible and self-controlled in a world that has gone crazy with sin, with the unrestrained indulgence of every fleshly desire, and the unrestrained expression of every emotion. We can let the Spirit of God dominate our minds and bring soundness, or we can let our own sinful natures dominate our minds and produce confusion and chaos. The choice is ours.

8
A Peaceful Mind

Troubled minds are the great plague of our times. Nearly 1 out of every 10 Americans seeks professional help for emotional distress. Some doctors estimate that better than 75 percent of their patients are suffering from symptoms that are induced by the effects of stress. North Americans spend over half a billion dollars a year on drugs to relieve their anxieties. Suicide ranks as the third leading cause of death among American teenagers. Anxiety is reaching epidemic proportions.

Did you know that anxiety is a sin? Any disobedience to the clear command of God's Word is sin, and His Word tells us not to worry. I am not calling attention to this for you to have something else to worry about. Please don't start worrying over the fact that you have been worrying lately. But one of the best ways to make progress in your Christian life is to first of all admit where you are spiritually and what you are from God's perspective; then you must absolutely refuse to rationalize sin. Here is the clearest statement in the Bible on the subject of a peaceful mind. "Be anxious for nothing, but in everything by prayer and supplication with thanksgiving let your requests be made known to God. And the peace of God, which surpasses all comprehension, shall guard your hearts and your minds in Christ Jesus" (Phil. 4:6-7).

The Prohibition

"Be anxious for nothing." This is not just a helpful suggestion, but a firm command. And *nothing* means just what it says, absolutely nothing. Don't worry about anything.

"You've got to be kidding," some people protest. "Nobody can live in this topsy-turvy world without worrying about anything at all. Paul must have had his head in the sand." No! He knew how difficult it was, and he knew how much Christians worry. In fact, he did a bit of worrying himself (cf. 2 Cor. 2:12-13). That was why he said, literally, "Stop worrying about anything." If this is the way God wants us to live, then we ought to examine it closely.

The word translated "be anxious" means, literally, "to draw in different directions" or "to be of a divided mind." It pictures harrassing, distressing, distracting thoughts that keep us tense, unsettled, and confused. It is the same word that Jesus used one day in Martha's house: "Martha, Martha, you are worried and bothered about so many things" (Luke 10:41). She was inwardly disturbed and agitated, hot and bothered. This is the kind of emotion that ties our stomachs in knots, puts deep wrinkles on our brows, raises our blood pressure, and makes us irritable and hard to get along with. Anxiety preys on our minds and keeps us from functioning normally. Jesus instructs us to never let anything get us into that frame of mind. Worrying does not accomplish one bit of good. It never solves any of our problems. It never improves our circumstances. I know that some people think it does. One lady said, "My *worrying* does work. Nothing I have ever worried about has ever come to pass." She was obviously trying to be funny. But rather than helping the situation, worrying hinders our ability to think constructively and act wisely. Jesus used this same word six times in one brief section of the Sermon on the Mount where He listed some of the things people are prone to worry about.

For this reason I say to you, do not be anxious for your life, as to what you shall eat, or what you shall drink;

nor for your body, as to what you shall put on. Is not life more than food, and the body than clothing? . . . And which of you by being anxious can add a single cubit to his life's span? And why are you anxious about clothing? Observe how the lilies of the field grow; they do not toil nor do they spin. . . . Do not be anxious then, saying "What shall we eat?" or "What shall we drink?" or "With what shall we clothe ourselves?". . . Therefore do not be anxious for tomorrow; for tomorrow will care for itself. Each day has enough trouble of its own (Matt. 6:25, 27-28, 31, 34).

Most of the things Christ mentioned could be summed up for us in one word—BILLS!! Money is one of our favorite things to worry about. "Do you know how much the cost of living is going to rise this year? We'll never find a place we can afford. We can't even afford to put groceries on the table. How are we ever going to make it?" Jesus said not to worry about things like that. Worrying reveals a basic lack of trust in God. It denies that God can take care of our needs, and so it belittles Him. In a sense, it is a subtle form of blasphemy because it speaks against God. Jesus said that our heavenly Father knows what we need and He will see that we get it (Matt. 6:32-33). Do you believe that? You cannot say you believe it, then turn around and worry. That would be totally inconsistent with your profession of faith in God.

Are you beginning to see why worry is a sin? Once again, the reason for establishing this point is not to add to your burden of guilt. It is to challenge you to admit that your worrying is sin so that you will confess it to God and experience His gracious forgiveness. You will never begin to get victory in this area until you acknowledge it as sin and receive the assurance of God's forgiveness. If you keep on excusing it, then you will just keep on worrying, living in a state of frenzy, feeling more guilty and emotionally distressed, and experiencing more physical symptoms all the time. You may be telling yourself that you have good reason to worry, but that will not eliminate its debilitating effects. The Apostle Paul wrote this for you. Stop worrying about anything!

Now it is one thing to know that worrying is wrong, but something entirely different to stop it. How many times have you said, "But I've tried to stop worrying and I can't"? Evidently you have not tried to stop by using God's way. He has a foolproof plan; it is 100 percent effective. Here is how to stop worrying.

The Plan

"In everything by prayer and supplication with thanksgiving let your requests be made known to God" (Phil. 4:6). The introductory words tell us *how* to do it, but *what* we are supposed to do is actually summed up in the statement: "Let your requests be made known to God." God's plan for us to overcome our anxieties is to present our requests to Him. Our *requests* are our petitions and our needs. "But doesn't God already know our needs?" Of course He does. Yet He asks us to make them known to Him, reveal them to Him. He wants us to come into His presence with an open heart and share the whole problem with Him just as though He didn't know anything about it. He wants us to express our confidence in Him by sharing that need in detail and by committing it to His care.

Incidentally, this is continuous action. We are to keep on making our requests known to Him. He never tires of hearing us tell Him about our needs and expressing to Him our total dependence on Him. Some folks say asking God repeatedly for the same things shows a lack of faith. But that is totally contrary to the universal testimony of Scripture. Jesus said, literally, that we should keep on asking, keep on seeking, and keep on knocking (Matt. 7:7). He told two parables—the friend at midnight (Luke 11:5-8), and the unjust judge (Luke 18:1-8)—to encourage persistency in bringing our requests to God. He wants us to keep coming. And He wants us to talk to Him about everything. This exhortation is prefaced by the words "in everything." We are to make our needs known

to God in every circumstance of life, all the time. Nothing
is too small for God's interest. Just as we are to worry about
nothing, so we are to talk to God about *everything*—all our
cares.

Somebody wrote:

It is God's will that I should cast
on Him my care each day;
He also bids me not to cast
my confidence away.

But, oh! I am so stupid, that
when taken unawares,
I cast away my confidence,
And carry all my cares.

Let's not be stupid anymore. Let's make our requests known
to God! But how are we to do it? There are three guiding
principles that help us understand the method by which we
are to reveal our needs to God. We approach Him by prayer,
by supplication, and with thanksgiving.

First, *by prayer*. There are several words for prayer in the
New Testament, and while some of them are used to refer to
requests directed to human beings, this one is used exclusively
to refer to our relationship with God. It is a general word for
prayer, emphasizing not so much our petitions and requests as
simply our communion and conversation with God. It is
prayer as an act of worship and devotion, just being in the
presence of God with an attitude of submissive adoration.

Do you see what Paul is saying here? God wants you to be
conscious of His presence all the time, aware that He is with
you and in control of every situation, as well as expressing
your devotion and submission to Him continually. In other
words, He wants your mind to be fixed on Him. He wants you
to let Him share every facet of your daily life. He wants you to
talk to Him about everything.

This is nothing new. Isaiah said the same thing about 800

years earlier. "Thou wilt keep him in perfect peace, whose mind is stayed on Thee, because he trusteth in Thee" (Isa. 26:3, KJV). The peaceful mind is the mind that is occupied with the Lord, that has learned to turn to Him immediately and automatically in every situation and talk to Him about everything. This will not happen without consciously cultivating a habit pattern. Memorizing and meditating on Scripture throughout the day will help us fix our minds on God. We need to ask Him first thing in the morning to help us do this throughout the day. By nightly evaluating our habit pattern of occupying our minds with the Lord, we will become aware of our areas of weakness. Then we can purpose daily to talk to Him about everything!

Second, *by supplication.* Here is another common New Testament word for prayer, this one emphasizing our need. It refers to a specific request for a specific need. If we want to get rid of worry, we need to present our requests to God, first by acknowledging His presence and allowing Him to be part of the situation, and then by zeroing in specifically on the problem at hand. We need to pray about the particular parts of the problem, and ask God to do explicit things which we believe would be within His will to do. In other words, we must *ask Him to meet every specific need.*

Most of our prayers are so general. "God, work this problem out," we pray. Well, God may not be ready to do that. He may have some important lessons to teach us through the course of working the problem out, lessons that can only be learned one step at a time. We need to try praying about one small part of the problem. Imagine, for example, a woman who has a stubborn husband and he refuses to admit that there is a problem in his marriage. He will not even talk about it. She becomes discouraged, depressed, anxious, and troubled. Finally, she cries out to God to do something, but she never asks Him for anything specific. What is it that she wants God to do besides waving a magic wand and making all her problems go away? Maybe she should ask God to help her be more patient and loving with her husband. That would help *her* to grow. But she has *needs* too. She could ask God to give her some indication that her husband loves her, or to help him come home in a good mood that day, or to cause him to be willing to talk about this particular problem. As God answers those requests, she can then move on to other specific things. We usually get into our problems one step at a time, and that is the way God usually brings us out of them. So we must learn to pray for one thing at a time. Specific answers to specific prayers will strengthen our faith and help us trust God for bigger things.

Third, *with thanksgiving*. Here is where many of us drop out of the game. We may be learning to cultivate a sense of God's presence and praying about every specific aspect of a problem, but we forget to encase our requests in thanksgiving. The plan is incomplete if we forget this third part of the formula. We will not stop worrying, and we will not enjoy the peaceful mind we desire.

We have many things to be thankful for, even when we feel as if our world is crumbling around us. We must thank God for who He is, for His loving care, for past blessings, and for the precious promises that relate to our present situation. We must thank Him for the problem itself (Eph. 5:20; cf. 1 Thes. 5:18). If we cannot think of any other reason for doing so, we must remember that it is another opportunity to grow stronger in God's grace, and thank Him for that. And thank Him ahead of time for what He is going to do. It may not be exactly what we would like Him to do, but it will be the best thing that could happen to us; so we can thank Him for whatever He does. There is great power in priase and thanksgiving. And it is not optional. It is an obligation. By making thanksgiving a regular part of our daily walk with God, we can *thank Him for everything*. If we follow the plan as God has revealed it, we will be ready for the promised blessing.

The Promise

"And the peace of God, which surpasses all comprehension, shall guard your hearts and your minds in Christ Jesus" (Phil.

4:7). This is a fantastic promise. "The peace of God"—that is, the perfect peace which finds its source in the God of all peace, a sense of inner rest, of contentment, tranquility, confidence, assurance, and happiness, a freedom from all anxious care—"shall guard your hearts and minds." *To guard* is a military expression meaning to keep watch, to guard or garrison. This is quite a picture. If we follow God's plan, then His battalion of peace will be stationed all around our minds, standing guard against every anxious thought, every temptation to worry, fret, or fear, against anything that would tend to harass us or distract us. Then we will be able to obey the prohibition. God will see to it! We will not worry about anything. And with our new peace of mind, we will save the money we might have had to spend on hospital bills, doctor bills, and drugstore bills. What a pleasant bonus!

Notice that God's peace will guard our *hearts* and *minds*. The heart often expresses the essential nature of man, including both his emotional and intellectual capacities. The heart often includes the functions of the mind. But then Paul mentions the mind itself, using a word that relates to thoughts, designs, or purposes, referring to the thinking faculty with which we work through the problems of life. The eternal, almighty God of the universe is going to protect our minds from all anxious care if we talk to Him about everything, ask Him to meet every specific need, and thank Him for whatever He does. His provision for a peaceful mind is there, waiting to be used. If we refuse to use it, we are denying the God we claim to know and trust, as dramatiized by this hypothetical conversation between two very smart birds:

> Said the Robin to the Sparrow,
> "I should really like to know
> Why these anxious human beings
> Rush about and worry so."
>
> Said the Sparrow to the Robin,
> "Friend, I think that it must be

> That they have no heavenly Father
> Such as cares for you and me."

We need to follow the plan and be a living testimony to those around us.

There is one other thing we need to mention. This peace that garrisons our minds is called a peace that surpasses all comprehension, and the word translated "comprehension" is actually the most common word for *mind* in the New Testament. Paul is calling God's peace quite literally, "a peace that surpasses the mind." A modern way of saying it could be, "It blows my mind." When God's peace is guarding our minds, it is more than the mind itself can conceive; it is beyond our human comprehension, surpassing our wildest dreams. It is a supernatural peace. I have heard Christians in times of deepest trial say to me, "I just can't believe the peace I've had through this problem." That is exactly the way the Christian life was intended to be lived.

If we Christians cannot understand it, the unbeliever will never be able to figure it out. He may even scoff, "Nobody can be that peaceful with that kind of problem. You need a psychiatrist!" But in spite of all the unbeliever's unkind accusations and insinuations, our supernatural peace will leave a deep impression on his soul that may eventually attract him to the Person of Jesus Christ, who alone can give him true peace as well.

My wife and I have seen God's plan work in our lives. I remember one occasion when the telephone awakened us at 3 A.M. It was an emergency-room nurse calling from a hospital in a neighboring town. She said, "Your son has been in an automobile accident and I suggest that you come right away."

I inquired, "How seriously is he injured?"

"I would just suggest that you come right away," she insisted.

As Mary and I drove the 15 miles to the hospital, we prayed aloud, committing Mark to the Lord, and thanking Him for whatever He was about to do. We had no idea whether our son was alive or dead, whether he would be a normal, functioning human being or a vegetable. But God gave us both a settled inner peace, the kind that defies explanation.

Mark and some other Christian friends had driven to Disneyland after work that evening, and we had given him permission to stay until it closed at 1 A.M. Then came the two-hour drive home. The driver had lost control of the car; and when it flipped over, Mark had been thrown through the window, with the car coming to rest just 18 inches from his head.

When we arrived at the emergency room, Mark was just regaining consciousness. His injuries were not critical and today the incident has almost been forgotten. But the memory of God's supernatural peace lives on. His plan works. I recommend it.

9
A Heavenly Mind

What do you want out of life? Have you ever clearly defined it? Nearly everybody is looking for something. Several years ago a Japanese firm conducted an international poll of 6,300 young people, ages 16-22, from 22 different countries in the world, including the United States. They were asked what they wanted most in life, and their answers revealed that the single most desired thing in the world for them is *money*! Is that what you want most?

Our Eternal Aims
God has something to say about what we should be seeking in life, what our aims and ambitions ought to be and how our priorities ought to be arranged. Here is how He led the Apostle Paul to express it: "If then you have been raised up with Christ, keep seeking the things above, where Christ is, seated at the right hand of God" (Col. 3:1).

Since we have been identified with Christ in His victory over sin and death, and in His resurrection to new life, we are to be seeking things above. That word *seek* means more than merely searching to find or discover something. It is earnestly desiring to have something and striving to obtain it. The word *seek* relates to purposes, goals, aims, and objectives. What is it that

Christians should be looking for in life? Paul says our goals are to be related to things above, where Christ is. Christ is seated at His Father's right hand in heaven, so our highest priorities in life ought to be things related to heaven!

That makes sense. Heaven is our home and our citizenship is there (Phil. 3:20). We are only temporary visitors to this planet, "aliens and strangers" as Peter described us (1 Peter 2:11, NIV). And someday the Lord Jesus is coming back to take us home (John 14:3). Why should our major goals be related to the earth when it is only a temporary stopping-off place for us? Why should we pour our energies, abilities, and resources into objectives that are tied to this world when we are going to leave it someday? That would be like visiting another country for a few months, working feverishly to get a job, building a house, establishing a bank account, seeking a measure of security, and then climbing on a airplane, flying home, and leaving everything we accumulated to somebody else. It would make far more sense to give that same degree of attention to our permanent home, which is what the Apostle Paul encourages us to do.

The Lord Jesus said much the same thing on two different occasions, one of which was a rather extended discourse on the subject of covetousness, or greed. "And do not seek what you shall eat, and what you shall drink, and do not keep worrying. For all these things the nations of the world eagerly seek; but your Father knows that you need these things. But seek for His kingdom, and these things shall be added to you" (Luke 12:29-31). He uses that word *seek* three times in these three short verses, and He tells us quite pointedly that the things we should want out of life as believers, the things we should earnestly desire and strive to obtain, ought to be things related to God's kingdom. Jesus is referring to *heaven* just as Paul was. That is clear from the conclusion of His lesson: "Sell your possessions and give to charity; make yourselves purses which do not wear out, an unfailing treasure in heaven, where no thief comes near, nor moth destroys" (Luke 12:33).

What does it mean to seek things related to heaven? It simply means to live for things that are eternal in nature. When we are seeking heavenly things, the most important matters in life for us are the things which last forever. Our aspirations and ambitions in this world are things we can go on enjoying in the next world as well. We have aims and objectives that are not limited to our short stay on earth, but rather we are dominated by the perspective we gain from our knowledge of Christ and His Word.

What perspective is that? Since heaven is a place of holiness, one of our aims is to grow in holiness. Since heaven is a place of fellowship with God, another goal is to cultivate our fellowship with Him now. Since our knowledge of God will be perfect in heaven, we want to get to know Him better right now in this life. Since Jesus Christ is glorified in heaven, we seek to glorify Him on earth. Since we shall be like Him in heaven, one of our great goals here on earth is to grow in His likeness, to develop Christlike qualities such as love, kindness, lowliness, meekness, unselfishness, patience, and forgiveness. Since the people we lead to a saving knowledge of Christ will be with us in heaven, soul-winning is a high priority in our life on earth. And these things take precedence over all other aims and ambitions.

The Earthbound Alternatives

These obviously are not the normal human goals. Most people have as their goals in life to get a job, find a mate, have a family, buy a home, accumulate some of the finer things of this world, and put enough money away for a comfortable retirement before they die. And that's about the extent of it. Their goals are related to the earth. This is a basic characteristic of unbelievers. They "set their minds on earthly things" (Phil. 3:19).

But, unfortunately, Christians can fall into the same trap. Living in an affluent society, they can allow the spirit of the age to affect their thinking. First, they want a spacious home in the suburbs, comfortably furnished, beautifully landscaped. Then a car, maybe two, or even three. Soon their needs expand, and what were once luxuries beyond their reach now become necessities they strive to obtain. Acquiring them becomes a major objective in life. The primary things on their minds are making more money, redecorating the house, adding on that extra room, and buying that fur coat, camper, boat, or sports car. Their attention is focused on the things of the world. They add one thing after another to their lists of acquisitions, but it seems as though there is always one more thing they would like to have, or think they need.

Vance Packard, in his book *The People Shapers,* claims that advertisers spend about $33 billion a year to keep the American consumer's passion for material things growing stronger. That averages out to nearly $600 per family per year. Their avowed goal is to give us an insatiable appetite for material comforts and to reshape our lifestyles, making us more hedonistic and status conscious. And the advertisers are succeeding beautifully, much to Satan's delight. Yet they are continually looking for new ways to get into our minds and mold our attitudes, carrying on elaborate scientific studies to identify the best prospects for each product, and making sophisticated electronic tests to measure the responses of various consumer groups to different advertising approaches.

It has been estimated that the average adult in the United States is hit with up to 500 advertising messages a day. The average young person sees approximately 20,000 television commercials a year; and by the time he is 18 years of age, he has seen and heard approximately 1,800 hours of commercials. It is estimated that mothers in the United States spend close to $4 billion extra a year at the urging of their TV-brainwashed children.

And if Satan cannot entice us with a direct appeal to our conscious minds, he will seek to bypass the conscious and make his subtle suggestions to the subconscious. Advertisers have been experimenting for years with subliminal techniques aimed at the subconscious mind (*subliminal* meaning "below the threshold," that is, the threshold of consciousness). These techniques are based on the fact that the brain is capable of receiving rapidly flashed images and low level sounds that the conscious mind does not detect.

Most people have heard of the now famous popcorn experiment conducted some years ago. A message hardly visible to the naked eye was quickly superimposed on the motion picture screen of a movie theater for a six-week period. It said, "Hungry? Eat popcorn." It was reported that popcorn sales increased over 50 percent during that period. There is nothing wrong with popcorn, but that experiment illustrates how subtly we can be motivated to do what somebody else wants us to do, and never know why.

A public outcry against subliminal techniques in the late 1950s and early 1960s slowed the advertisers down; but investigations have continued, new methods have been developed, and further experiments have been conducted both in theaters and on television. There are still very few laws regulating their use, and it is quite likely that Christians will have to reckon with the subtle pressures of advertisers in years to come.

And now, two-way cable TV that makes it possible for the consumer to respond to a high pressure sales pitch immediately, before he has had a chance to cool off and think it over. All he has to do is push three or four buttons on the console in his living room and that glittering new gadget he thinks he needs so badly will be at his door in the morning. And of course, he can pay for it later.

Just think how convenient it will be to get all those neat things he wants, and how easy it will be to go bankrupt!

The result of all this is that in America we squander more resources and throw away more merchandise than much of the world has to use in the first place. Somebody has estimated that we demand 21 tons of mineral materials per person each year in this country to provide the food, shelter, transportation, and manufactured goods we use. Just making these materials usable requires another 8,300 pounds of petroleum per person per year, 5,300 pounds of coal, and 5,000 pounds of natural gas.

And then there is the matter of food. Our garbage disposals may eat better than 30 percent of the world's population eats. Each resident of the United States requires 2,000 pounds of grain a year, most of which goes to produce the meat and dairy products he likes so much. By contrast, some countries feed their populations on 400 pounds of grain per person each year. To the rest of the world, the American must look like a selfish child in a room full of toys, grabbing as many as he can get and piling them up in his own little corner. Where will it end?

Many experts are predicting that we Americans will be forced to adopt a drastically simpler lifestyle. That will be difficult for us to accept unless we get back to biblical perspectives on material things. Jesus said it so beautifully. It came in answer to a man who wanted Jesus to make his brother share the inheritance with him: "And he said unto them, 'Take heed, and beware of covetousness; for a man's life consisteth not in the abundance of the things which he possesseth" (Luke 12:15, KJV).

Covetousness is simply desiring more for ourselves. It may be something we want very much, or something somebody else has, or something we think we justly deserve. But our minds are set on acquiring it. We are convinced that if only we can get it, our lives will somehow be more happy, complete, and fulfilled; and we will be more significant as persons. So we keep on acquiring one thing after another, but, oddly enough, we do not seem to feel any happier or any more significant. We get everything we want, but for some strange reason, we don't want anything we have. Instead, we are bored with it all. That is because the eternal, indisputable, inviolable Word of God says that real living does not consist in the abundance of things which we possess! Material things can never satisfy the longing within us. In all of life, that seems to be one of the most difficult lessons we have to learn.

The Lord Jesus illustrated His point with a story about a wealthy farmer who had such a good year he could not find enough barn space in which to store his grain. God had been good to him; yet he never acknowledged that God was responsible for his prosperity, nor did he ever seek God's guidance about what to do with his extra assets. God might have told him to donate to the temple or give to the poor, and he did not want to hear that. He wanted to hoard all his extra assets for his own future use. He said to himself, "You have plenty of good things laid up for many years. Take life easy; eat, drink, and be merry." God's response must have jolted his smug, self-confident mind: "You fool! This very night your life will be demanded from you. Then who will get what you have prepared for yourself?" (Luke 12:19-20, NIV)

This man acted stupidly. He spent a lifetime accumulating material things which he never got to enjoy. We are never told whether or not he was a believer; we do not know whether he woke up in heaven or hell. But one thing was certain—wherever he was, he did not have his material goods with him. And neither shall we.

Most of us Christians are very much like our unsaved neighbors. Like them, we live in lavish houses, drive expensive cars, wear fashionable clothes, dine in the same exclusive restaurants, and enjoy most of the same luxuries. But someday we will awake in eternity stripped of all our earthly possessions, just exactly as they will. And someone else will be using all the junk we amassed on earth, after the federal government and the state government have gotten their share, and our heirs have finished hassling over the rest. And what will all of our earthly possessions count for then? Absolutely nothing!

The Effective Answer

God has given us the answer. "Set your minds on things above, not on earthly things" (Col. 3:2, NIV). *Seeking* things above (v. 1) has to do with the goals we actively pursue. But *setting our minds* on things above (v. 2) has to do with what we think about. And what we think about is actually the key to goal-setting. Our goals in life are going to grow out of what we occupy our minds with; so the way to seek the right things is to set our minds on the right things. The solution to our struggle with materialism—the only safeguard against seeking things on earth—is to fix our attention on things above. We need to think heaven, to be heavenly minded.

I realize the idea of a heavenly mind has been greatly disparaged. We have all heard of people who are so heavenly minded, they're of no earthly good. By that I mean they seem to be a little bit flaky, other worldly, preoccupied, and out of touch with reality; or maybe so "super-spiritual" that they do not know what is going on in the real world. They cannot relate to real people and their needs in real life. That is obviously no way for children of God to live, but living this way has no relationship whatsoever to the exhortation of this verse. Satan has a way of twisting a good idea around and making it appear so ridiculous that everybody will dismiss it as invalid. God says we are to think heaven; and when we are heavenly minded in the true biblical sense of the term, it affects everything we do in this real world—absolutely everything! What we think about will eventually control the totality of our lives on earth. If we want to have objectives and goals with eternal value, we will need to think about eternal things:

- think about the Lord—who He is, what He is like, how He deals with us, and what He expects of us;
- think about His Word—what it means and how it applies to our lives;
- memorize Scripture, meditate on it, let it occupy our thoughts;
- approach every situation in life with a desire to do God's will, looking for the guidance which His Word offers.

When we find ourselves thinking wistfully of material things, we should ask, "What has all this got to do with eternity?" Our whole lifestyle would change dramatically if we began to ask that question of ourselves regularly.

That is not to say we will never buy another modern convenience. But we will weigh every purchase in the light of eternity. Before we buy anything consequential, we will each ask ourselves: "Is this something God wants me to have, or does He have some better way for me to spend this money? Will this have any significance by eternity's standards? Will this contribute to the glory of God, the salvation of souls, or the spiritual strength of God's people?"

Scripture does say that God gives us richly all things to enjoy (1 Tim. 6:17), but that is not to say that we have the right to buy anything our hearts desire. That statement was not made to justify buying everything we think we can afford without consulting the Lord about it. The Lord is the One who has given us the health, the strength, the ability, and the opportunity to earn the money we have. Ultimately, it all comes from Him. We are merely stewards entrusted with the management of His resources, and we should check with Him before we spend any of His money. Occupying our minds with thoughts of the Lord and His Word will help us remember to do that consistently.

It will also help us to keep our priorities straight. It is so easy to put making money higher on our priority list than God wants it to be. Some folks have placed their jobs before everything else in life for the security of having more money, for the prestige of advancement, for the power of controlling people, or possibly for the enjoyment of an image of success and prosperity before their friends. But their jobs rob them of the time they need to get to know God, to meet the emotional and spiritual needs of their families, and to serve Jesus Christ through the local church to which He has led them. Their jobs have taken over their lives.

Most people who have fallen into that trap insist that they will get their priorities straightened out as soon as they reach a certain level of security. But it seldom happens that way. There is little hope of significant changes being made until they learn to occupy their minds with things above, with things of eternal value—until they develop heavenly minds. High blood pressure, heart attacks, and bleeding ulcers have helped some people decide to put the Lord and their families before their jobs. But that is the hard way. It would be so much easier for them simply to make that decision now, while it is fresh in their minds.

God puts us on this earth to do His will, and He has stated very plainly that it is not His will for us to amass money and material goods for ourselves. From a biblical perspective, our secular jobs are for the purpose of supporting us and our families while we serve the Lord, minister to other believers (inside our families as well as outside), and share the Gospel with a lost world. Our jobs also provide us with money to give to God's work and to people in need. But our jobs are not to be the major thing in our lives. Suppose we do make it to the top of our company, our profession, or our trade. What will that have to do with eternity?

This chapter began with a question: "What do you want out of life? What are you really looking for?" The right answer for the child of God is, "I want to glorify God with my life by doing His will." The only way you will be able to give that answer honestly is by beginning to set your mind on things above, not on earthly things.

10
All Your Mind

Did you ever say to someone, "I love you with all my heart"? What did you mean when you said it? What did those words convey? Try to remember. It is important to the understanding of your relationship with God.

To love someone with all your heart is to love with a total love that surpasses our love for anyone or anything else, a love that affects your total being—your mind, emotions, and will. Total loving directs your thoughts, dominates your feelings, and determines your actions. It supersedes all other loves, and it causes you to give unselfishly of yourself for the sake of the one you love, to put all you are and all you have into that relationship. It involves your whole personality and governs the whole disposition of your life. It is unreserved and undiluted devotion.

It is far easier to *say* you love somebody with all your heart than it is to *do* it. Yet that is the ideal toward which you should be growing. On the human level, that degree of devotion is usually reserved for a husband or wife. But there is another level that transcends the human. The Scriptures clearly call on you to let your relationship with God fully engage your entire being—your whole heart.

We all know that the heart is technically an organ that

pumps life-supporting blood to every cell in the body. But when we say something like, "I love you with all my heart," we are using the word *heart* figuratively to describe our inner person. That is exactly what the Hebrew people in Israel's early history did, but even to a greater extent than we do. To them the heart was the center of a person's being, the seat of the intelligence, the hub of the emotions, the focal point of the will, the source of all thought, all feeling, and all action. The heart embraced the whole inner person. It was the control center of the life.

The more we study this figurative use of the word *heart* in Scripture, the more we realize that it is located between the ears rather than between the armpits. It is the same thing we refer to as the *mind*. In a symbolic sense, the heart has thoughts and intentions (Gen. 6:5; Ps. 14:1; Heb. 4:12). It meditates (Ps. 19:14). It considers (Deut. 8:5). It desires (Ps. 37:4). It stores God's Word (Ps. 119:11). It can be wise, or skillful (Ex. 31:6). It can be willing (Ex. 35:5). It can be deceitful (Jer. 17:9).

There is not much question that when the Hebrews spoke of the heart, they were frequently referring to what we know as the mind. In fact, there is no specific word for mind used in the entire Old Testament. The word that means "purpose, device, or imagination" is once translated "mind" in the King James Version (*yetser*, Isa. 26:3), as is the word for "mouth" (*peh*, Lev. 24:12). The word that means "life, breath, or soul" is sometimes translated "mind" (*nephesh, e.g.,* Gen. 23:8), and so is the word for "spirit" (*ruach, e.g.,* Prov. 29:11). But the most frequent words rendered "mind" in the Old Testament are the words for the heart (*leb, lebab*).

When the Hebrews spoke of doing something with all their hearts, they meant putting their whole beings, and especially, their whole minds to it. And they knew that their relationship with the Lord demanded that level of commitment, whether or not they ever attained it. Solomon probably said it best: "Let your heart therefore be wholly devoted to the Lord our God" (1 Kings 8:61). He was calling for wholehearted commitment to God and single-minded sincerity in their devotion to Him.

But so far we have been speaking in generalities. To what specific areas does God want us to apply our minds fully and completely? The Book of Deuteronomy provides the clearest answers. And the first area is the most important. If we understand and apply ourselves to this first area, the other areas will become developed as a natural outgrowth.

Love God with All Your Mind

The Jewish worship service centered around what they called the Shema (pronounced Sh'mah). The word *Shema* is the imperative form of the verb "to hear" and is the first word in Deuteronomy 6:4: "Hear, O Israel! The Lord is our God, the Lord is One!" The full Shema included Deuteronomy 6:4-9; Deuteronomy 11:13-21; and Numbers 15:37-41. Little leather boxes called *phylacteries* contained the Shema. The Jews wore the phylacteries on the forehead or wrist during prayer. They also placed the Shema in small cylindrical boxes which were affixed to the doors of their homes. The Jews obviously considered the opening statement of the Shema, asserting that our Lord is One, to be extremely important. And the Lord Jesus agreed. When He was asked by a lawyer what He considered the first and greatest commandment to be, He introduced His comments by quoting that opening statement (cf. Mark 12:29-31).

But as Jesus pointed out, the Shema contained these words: "And you shall love the Lord your God with all your heart and with all your soul and with all your might" (Deut. 6:5). It is interesting, however, that when Christ quoted this to the lawyer, He added the mind. He told the lawyer to love God with all his heart, soul, *mind,* and strength (Mark 12:30), as if to reiterate that the mind is an indispensable element in that Old Testament concept of the heart. He was to put his whole mind into loving God—the most important commandment in the entire Bible.

Some people dislike emphasizing the mind in their relationship with God. They like to distinguish "head knowledge" from "heart knowledge," and often refer to the 18 inches between the head and the heart as being the distance between heaven and hell. It is certainly possible to have an intellectual familiarity with the Gospel without committing oneself to it in saving faith. But to be perfectly accurate, the organ in the chest that pumps blood cannot believe anything. Faith takes place in the head—in the mind, the center of man's thoughts, feelings, and will. All three elements are involved when someone truly believes, and that is what it means, scripturally, to believe with the heart (as in Romans 10:9-10).

All three are also involved when we love God with all our hearts. We apply our intellect to acquiring knowledge about God and growing in our personal acquaintance with Him. This in turn affects our emotions, arousing feelings of pleasure, confidence, assurance, enthusiasm, warm attachment, affection, tenderness, and devotion. And we willfully choose to act in a manner which we know will please Him. This process becomes so important to us that we put our entire beings into it. We enjoy getting into the Word and learning more about Him. We love to cultivate those tender feelings we have toward Him. And we take pleasure in doing what He wants us to do. This process is the most important thing in our lives. It takes precedence over everything else.

It is doubtful that there are very many Christians who love God that much. Many of us put other people in the place that should be reserved for God alone. We apply more of our energies to making money, acquiring things, and having fun than we do to knowing and loving God. And that fact probably accounts for much of the unhappiness in our lives. If something else comes before God in our affections, and we fail to achieve what we have grown to love, or lose it after we have achieved it, life has no more meaning for us. We become discouraged and depressed. But if our affections are set on God above all else, the loss of earthly things or human loved ones only drives us closer to Him, enlarges our knowledge of Him, increases our love for Him, and thus enhances the meaning of life.

Not many people believe or are willing to try this philosophy. They are afraid it will not work. But God would never have asked us to put Him first if He had known it would not work. We shouldn't be like the double-minded man whom James described (James 1:8). His divided mind led to a lack of stability and consistency in every area of his life. We need to establish as our major priority in life: growing in our knowledge of God; growing in our love for him; and, giving ourselves to this task wholly.

Seek God with All Your Mind

Maybe we will have to admit that we have had our minds focused on other things and on other people. Our love for the Lord may not even have entered our thoughts for days or weeks at a time. We have gotten absorbed in other pursuits and, in a sense, they have become our gods. If that is the case, the consequences have not been pleasant; for feelings of guilt, worthlessness, emptiness, dissatisfaction, and discouragement often follow when our love for God grows cool. Where do we go from here?

We can be assured that God was not taken by surprise when we left our first love. He knew we would do it, just as he knew His Old Testament people the Israelites would do it. He told them that they would be tempted to serve other gods, and He warned them that they would be uprooted from their land and scattered among the nations if they did so (cf. Deut. 4:25-28). Then He went on to explain what they should do when that happened. "But from there you will *seek* the Lord your God, and you will find Him if you search for Him with all your heart and all your soul" (Deut. 4:29). They were to seek Him with all their minds. But what did that mean?

God said much the same thing to the people of Jeremiah's day. He warned them of the Babylonian Captivity, and then said, "And you will seek Me and find Me, when you search for Me with all your heart" (Jer. 29:13). This verse is not from a Gospel text. I can remember an enthusiastic new believer who stumbled onto this verse shortly after his salvation and proceeded to alienate all his family and friends with it, urging them to cry out to God and plead with all their hearts for Him to save them. The simple acknowledgment of sin, and simple faith in the sacrifice of Christ on Calvary's Cross is sufficient to secure eternal salvation. There is no need to beg God with all our hearts.

This verse was written to God's wayward people. He wanted them to acknowledge their sin and turn back to Him with all their hearts. He was not hiding Himself from them. But He did want to see a genuine spirit of repentance and a wholehearted desire to honor Him with their lives.

God makes Himself readily accessible to us, but He does want us to seek Him wholeheartedly. He does not enjoy watching us suffer the consequences of our stubbornness, rebellion, and waywardness. He has a beautiful future planned for us. " 'For I know the plans that I have for you,' declares the Lord, 'plans for welfare and not for calamity to give you a future and a hope' " (Jer. 29:11). So we need to turn to Him, talk to Him, and acknowledge our sins. He is ready to listen (cf. Jer. 29:12). He is willing to forgive, restore, and bless (cf. Jer. 29:14). But He does not want a halfhearted admission of guilt, a hypocritical turning from sin, or a lukewarm effort at prayer. He wants us to seek Him with all our minds.

Serve God with All Your Mind

If we love someone with all our minds, then we are obviously going to live for that person's good. And that is what God asks of His people. "And now, O Israel, what does the Lord your God ask of you but to fear the Lord your God, to walk in all His ways, to love Him, to serve the Lord your God with all your heart and with all your soul" (Deut. 10:12, NIV; cf. also 11:13). The essence of the matter is: For whom are we living? Who has our loyalty, devotion, and allegiance?

Serving the Lord is contrasted, in the Old Testament, to serving other gods. Joshua challenged the people of his day, saying, "But if serving the Lord seems undesirable to you, then choose for yourselves this day whom you will serve, whether the gods your forefathers served beyond the river, or the gods of the Amorites, in whose land you are living. But as for me and my household, we will serve the Lord" (Josh. 24;15, NIV). They obviously could not live their lives for God and for pagan idols at the same time. They had to worship and serve one or the other. St. Augustine suggested that man is incurably worshipful. He is going to worship some god. If it is not the Lord God, then it will probably be material things, or maybe even himself.

As Jesus said, "No one can serve two masters. Either he will hate the one and love the other, or he will be devoted to the one and despise the other. You cannot serve both God and Money" (Matt. 6:24, NIV). In that statement He put His finger on the heart of the problem in our day. Normally, for us, the problem is not declaring allegiance to some pagan idol. Rather, it is living for money, material possessions, and financial security. It is serving the god of greed. Most professing Christians appear to be serving the Lord. But their other god keeps demanding more and more of their time and energies. Their desire for present comforts and future security interferes with their loyalty to Jesus Christ; and their minds are pulled in two directions, causing conflict, deceitfulness, guilt, and sometimes, depression.

The only solution to that dilemma is to make a choice. If we are going to serve the Lord, then we will have to decide to serve Him with *all* our minds. When we begin to think about what He has done for us, that is the only sensible decision to make. That is the way Samuel approached the problem with the people of his day. "Only fear the Lord, and serve Him in truth with all your heart; for consider how great things He has done for you" (1 Sam. 12:24, KJV).

Obey the Lord with All Your Mind

If we have our priorities properly arranged in our minds, and our love for the Lord takes precedence over everything else, then we will obviously obey Him with all our minds. "The

Lord your God commands you this day to follow these decrees and laws; carefully observe them with all your heart and with all your soul" (Deut. 26:16, NIV).

In Scripture, love for God is often linked to obedience. For example, Jesus said, "If you love Me, you will obey what I command" (John 14:15, NIV). John added his inspired thoughts: "This is love for God: to obey His commands" (1 John 5:3, NIV). That is so logical and reasonable that it hardly requires explanation. If we love Him we will want what is best for Him. He certainly knows what is best for Him, and He has explained it to us in His Word. So if we really love Him, we are going to live as His Word tells us to live. This is the most tangible expression of love we can offer to Him who loves us so ultimately.

But we humans are such illogical and unreasonable creatures. We insist that we love God; yet when our desires conflict with His, we often choose our own way and use some clever rationalization to justify our actions. For example, the man who wants to divorce his wife, with no biblical cause, will explain away the passages that forbid him. Yet he goes on protesting his love for God. That is deceitful. If he loves Him with all his heart, he will pour his whole being into living as God's Word requires. He will obey Him with all his mind, regardless of what his desire might be.

And the rewards will be immense. Here is what God promised to Israel: "Then the Lord your God will prosper you abundantly in all the work of your hand, in the offspring of your body and in the offspring of your cattle and in the produce of your ground, for the Lord will again rejoice over you for good, just as He rejoiced over your fathers; if you obey the Lord your God to keep His commandments and His statutes which are written in this book of the Law, if you turn to the Lord your God with all your heart and soul" (Deut. 30:9-10). But whether or not He prospers us materially, we will experience abundant blessing that can be enjoyed in no other way. We will have the satisfaction of being in a right relationship with the eternal God. There will be freedom from guilt and fear, an inner peace and contentment, genuine and lasting joy, and a real purpose in living.

What are we waiting for? Let's start pursuing our relationship with God with all our minds. "For the eyes of the Lord move to and fro throughout the earth that He may strongly support those whose heart is completely His" (2 Chron. 16:9).

II
A Willing
Mind

Has anyone ever told you that you were stubborn? Most of us have a stubborn streak in us, and somebody usually musters up the courage to point it out to us somewhere along the way. But we love to make excuses for our stubbornness, don't we? One of our favorites seems to be blaming it on our ancestors. "I'm German, or I'm Dutch, or I'm some other nationality; that's why I'm so stubborn." So we go on our merry ways, persistently ignoring other people's opinions, feelings, and needs; tenaciously following our own courses of action in spite of reasons, arguments, or persuasions to the contrary; and refusing to give in to others on any issue. We are right, though the whole world be wrong. We may even refuse to give in to God.

Stubbornness is a mental attitude, a mind-set. We are obstinate toward others and resistant to change because we choose to be. Our reasons may be pride, self-centeredness, desire for personal convenience, insecurity, lack of self-esteem, love of sin, or any number of other things. But stubbornness is still an attitude which we choose in our own minds. And it is totally contrary to the mind of God's Spirit.

There is a distinct emphasis in Scripture on a willing mind, a mind that is open to God's thoughts, ready to do His will, and eager to please Him rather than stubbornly being set on its own way. Let's explore some specific biblical areas in which God wants us to have a willing mind. The first one is found in the Book of Nehemiah.

Willing to Work for the Lord

The Book of Nehemiah is about building. God burdened Nehemiah, the cupbearer of the Persian king, with the tremendous task of rebuilding the walls of Jerusalem. Those broken-down walls were an open invitation to the enemies of God's people to attack the city. Furthermore, the piles of rubbish and trash from the ruins were keeping their morale at low ebb. City walls were a symbol of solidarity, security, and systematic living. Without them, life was in danger and disarray. So Nehemiah arrived in Jerusalem in 445 B.C. with a mandate from the Persian king to rebuild those walls. Let him tell his own story.

> Then I said to them, "You see the bad situation we are in, that Jerusalem is desolate and its gates burned by fire. Come, let us rebuild the wall of Jerusalem that we may no longer be a reproach."
> And I told them how the hand of my God had been favorable to me, and also about the king's words which he had spoken to me. Then they said, "Let us arise and build." So they put their hands to the good work (Neh. 2:17-18).

It was a good work because it was God's work. Building broken-down walls does not sound exceptionally spiritual. But if God wanted it done, then it was His work. Even building walls can be a spiritual ministry if God directs it. But the going was tough. All the rubble had to be cleared away by hand. No bulldozers or dump trucks were available to make the work easier. Beside that, jealous pagan neighbors taunted the Jews and threatened to attack them. But they worked faithfully and diligently. There were 42 separate crews. Each worker was assigned to the portion of the wall nearest to his own home. Each was working shoulder to shoulder, praying as he labored, and watching for his enemies day and night (Neh. 4:9).

"So we built the wall and the whole wall was joined together to half its height, for the people had a mind to work" (Neh. 4:6). Again, the word *mind* is actually the Hebrew word for heart; but as we have seen, the Jews used the heart to describe the center of man's reasoning faculties. These people thought through the issues and became convinced that they ought to do the will of God even though it would demand strenuous physical effort and back-breaking work. They had a mind to work.

Not that all people in Jerusalem wanted to work, for "their nobles would not put their shoulders to the work" (Neh. 3:5, NIV). Perhaps they reasoned that those walls weren't necessary. After all, it had been 93 years since the first contingent of exiles had returned to Jerusalem and they had lived without walls all that time. I can hear them complaining: "Look, Nehemiah. We've gotten along just fine without walls for nearly a century. So what makes it so important now? It's not worth the effort. Forget it. You don't realize how big a job this is going to be. Besides, it's not fair for us nobles to have to do this manual labor." It did not matter what God had said. They stubbornly resisted. The rest of the people just ignored them and kept right on working. They had a mind that was willing to work for the Lord.

People have not changed much in 2,500 years. There are still some with a mind to work and others who balk at every new job that needs to be done. "That's too much like work," they grumble. "Count me out. I'd rather pay somebody to do it." If they have the money to pay somebody, they could give it to missions and come out and help anyway. Often, when something needs to be done for the Lord, people say that their first obligation is to their secular job. That would seem to be an acceptable excuse, especially when they are following biblical principles for handling their finances. But lots of times, people just don't want to be bothered, or don't want anything to interfere with their own selfish plans. They probably have not yet allowed the Lord to deal with their stubbornness and give them a willing mind. These people need to prayerfully cultivate a mind-set that is open and eager to do God's work.

Willing to Give to the Lord

Another great Old Testament illustration of a willing mind is found in the Book of Exodus. God was talking with Moses on Mt. Sinai. "Speak unto the children of Israel, that they bring Me an offering: of every man that giveth it willingly with his heart you shall take My offering" (Ex. 25:2, KJV). The building of the tabernacle would obviously necessitate a large supply of materials: metals, fabrics, animal skins, spices, and precious stones. There were no lumberyards, hardware stores, fabric centers, or gem shops in the wilderness; so the only source of supply would be what the people themselves actually owned. But God did not want them to give unless they could do so with a willing mind, without coercion and without reluctance. He wanted His people to give with a *joyfully ready mind.*

Look at this illustration again as Moses relates God's intructions to the people: "Take from among you a contribution to the Lord; whoever is of a willing heart, let him bring it as the Lord's contribution: gold, silver, and bronze (Ex. 35:5). He emphasized again that the offering had to be given with a willing mind. And that is exactly how the people gave. "And they came, both men and women, as many as were willing-hearted. . . . The children of Israel brought a willing offering unto the Lord, every man and woman, whose heart made them willing to bring for all manner of work, which the Lord had commanded to be made by the hand of Moses" (Ex. 35:22, 29, KJV). The results were overwhelming. "And they spoke unto Moses, saying, 'The people bring much more than enough for the service of the work, which the Lord commanded to make' " (Ex. 36:5, KJV).

The same thing happened when David gathered materials for Solomon to use in building the temple. After David explained what he himself had given, he asked, "Who then is willing to consecrate himself this day to the Lord?" (1 Chron. 29:5) The people responded enthusiastically. "Then the rulers of the fathers' households, and the princes of the tribes of Israel, and the commanders of thousands and of hundreds, with the overseers over the king's work, offered willingly; and for the service for the house of God they gave. . . . Then the people rejoiced because they had offered so willingly, for they made their offering to the Lord with a whole heart, and King David also rejoiced greatly" (1 Chron. 29:6-9).

Years later, when King Hezekiah led his people in a great revival, cleansed the temple, and restored its worship, we can find the same emphasis. The king encouraged the people who had consecrated themselves to the Lord to bring sacrifices and thank offerings to His house. "And the congregation brought in sacrifices and thank offerings; and as many as were of a free heart burnt offerings" (2 Chron. 29:31, KJV). The words *free heart* are the same ones we have seen before, meaning "a willing mind." These Old Testament believers had minds that were willing to give to the Lord.

One thing that causes many of us to stiffen our backs in stubborn resistance is when somebody messes around with our wallets. We balk at that quicker than almost anything, clutching our money selfishly and bucking anybody who tries to tell us what to do with it. That wallet can become an obstacle to a life of total surrender, and the symbol of our subtle rebellion against God and of our reluctance to do His will.

The Corinthians had that problem. They had promised Paul they would give generously for the poverty-stricken believers in Jerusalem, and they did begin to carry out their promise. But when it was time to complete the job, they resisted. They probably said something like, "We can't give it, Paul. It's too much of a hardship on us. We just don't have it." That is why Paul said, "Now therefore perform the doing of it; that as there was a readiness to will, so there may be a performance also out of that which you have. For if there be first a willing mind, it is accepted according to that a man has, and not according to that he has not" (2 Cor. 8:11-12, KJV). The word translated "readiness" in the first sentence is the same word translated "a willing mind" in the second. Paul wanted more than just money from the Corinthians. He wanted them to have minds that were *willing* to give as well.

And God wants the same from us today. He does not want our money if we give it grudgingly. He wants to see a joyful and enthusiastic readiness to share our possessions in His work. He does not expect us to give what we do not have. While we may need to restructure our priorities and rethink our true needs so that we have more to give, God is delighted to receive whatever we are able to give if the willingness is there. The key to biblical giving is a willing mind.

Willing to Receive the Word

The third kind of willing mind we want to consider is found in the Book of Acts. Paul and Silas had just left Thessalonica. Some of the Jews there, along with a great multitude of Greeks and a number of prominent women, had trusted Christ as Saviour, and the unbelieving Jews were infuriated. They stirred up quite a disturbance, and the Christians considered it wise to get Paul and Silas out of town. "And the brethren immediately sent away Paul and Silas by night unto Berea; who, coming there, went into the synagogue of the Jews. These were more noble than those in Thessalonica, in that they received the Word with all readiness of mind, and searched the Scriptures daily, whether those things were so" (Acts 17:10-11, KJV).

The Jews in the synagogue at Berea were literally more *noble-minded* than those in Thessalonica. They had loftier thoughts. Why? Because they received the Word of God with readiness of mind, that is, with *willing minds*. That is the same word we have just seen applied to the Corinthians. The Jews in Thessalonica let pride and prejudice keep them from considering these new ideas Paul expounded. But the Jews in Berea were open-minded, willing to consider the truth and to receive it.

It is so easy to let our traditional ideas obscure what the Word of God actually says. Sometimes we hear a Bible expositor suggest something contrary to our pet theories and we bristle with stubborn resistance. "That's not the way my grandfather believed it, and it's not the way my father believed it, and I'll never believe it that way." Or we may say, "We've never understood it that way around here. And we don't see any reason to consider changing our minds now." The noble Bereans had open minds. Willing minds are open minds, unbiased by preconceived notions, ready to be taught by God's Spirit.

But the nobility of the Bereans was not only in that they were open to new ideas. It was also in that they evaluated what Paul said in the light of the Scriptures to see if it were true. They searched the Scriptures in a careful and exact manner, as one would search a legal document. They tested everything Paul said by God's Word. You see, these Bereans were not gullible. Being open-minded did not mean they swallowed every new doctrine that came along. People can get led astray that way. But not the Bereans—they measured everything against the standard of the Word, as we must do.

Willing minds do not accept everything they hear. They listen without prejudgment, then they go to the Word to test what they have heard. This requires a delicate balance and extreme care. We are doomed to spiritual stagnation if we close our minds to new ideas. Some churches have lost their power because they have been unalterably tied to traditional ways of thinking and acting. But we are likewise doomed if we uncritically embrace every new thing we hear. Other churches have lost their testimony by accepting new doctrines which contradict the Scriptures. We need willing minds like the Bereans had, minds that are open to new ideas but anchored to God's infallible Word.

Willing to Share the Gospel

The Apostle Paul himself was an example of another facet of the willing mind. He had never visited the city of Rome when he wrote to the believers there, yet in his letter, he reveals an intimate acquaintance with many of them. Some were his own converts who had subsequently moved to Rome. Paul longed to visit them. One of his great ambitions was to preach the Gospel in the hub of the Roman empire. "And I do not want you to be unaware, brethren, that often I have planned to come to you (and have been prevented thus far) in order that I might obtain some fruit among you also, even as among the rest of the Gentiles. I am under obligation both to Greeks and to barbarians, both to the wise and to the foolish. Thus, for my part, I am eager to preach the Gospel to you also who are in Rome" (Rom. 1:13-15).

The word *eager* is the adjective form of the same word we have seen in both Acts 17 and in 2 Corinthians 8. Paul is saying, "I have a willing mind. I am ready to preach the Gospel wherever God wants me to preach it. And I believe He wants me to preach it in Rome. I'm willing to go."

Rome would not be the safest place for Paul to visit. There was a growing resentment against Christians there, particularly as the Roman emperors began to demand worship as gods. That was an act of homage which Christians were not prepared to offer, and many were about to suffer for their devotion to Christ. But the fiery little apostle could not wait to get there. He saw himself as a debtor. He owed it to the unbelieving world to share the joy of forgiveness in Christ. He was not ashamed of the message he preached. It was God's power unto eternal salvation (Rom. 1:16). And he was ready to share it anywhere, even if he had to suffer for it. That is the willing mind God wants all of us to have.

Some professing Christians balk at this: "I don't believe in talking about my faith. It's a personal, private thing. And besides that, I don't want to appear as though I'm pushing my religion on anyone else." It is hard to imagine a true believer saying these words. If he really knows that his sins are forgiven and that heaven is assured; if he has experienced the satisfaction of a personal relationship with Jesus Christ; and if he is enjoying the fullness of life in Christ; it would seem

A Willing Mind / 111

likely that he would want others to share the same happiness. It would seem that he might even have a difficult time being quiet about it. If he really believes that unsaved people will experience eternal torment, it would seem normal to warn them. In fact, according to this passage of Scripture, he *owes* that to them. Aren't you glad the person who told you the Gospel was not stubborn about sharing it?

To be available as God's mouthpieces, begin every day by saying something like, "Lord, I'm ready to share the Gospel with anybody You lead me to today. You open the doors, and I'll walk through them." That is a willing mind.

Willing to Live Holy Lives

The Lord Jesus taught His three sleepy disciples in the garden of Gethsemane a lesson about the willing mind. He had asked them to pray with Him, but they had dozed off to sleep. "And He came to the disciples and found them sleeping, and said to Peter, 'So, you men could not keep watch with Me for one hour? Keep watching and praying, that you may not enter into temptation; the spirit is willing, but the flesh is weak'" (Matt. 26:40-41). They would need divine strength to withstand the immense pressures to which they would be subjected in the hours and days to come. The only way they could find that strength would be through prayer. Without it, their human spirits were sure to be overcome by the impulses of the flesh.

But did you notice the word *willing?* Jesus said, "The spirit is willing." That is the same word we have been looking at in other passages. It means "a willing mind." What a great principle we have here! The human spirit may be willing to overcome temptation and do what God desires, we may have a mind-set that is willing to live a holy life, but that in itself is not enough. We also have those old sinful inclinations that are a part of the flesh and the flesh seeks to gratify only itself. The flesh cannot please God (cf. Rom. 7:18; 8:8). We need a mind that is willing to live a godly life, but we also need to lay hold of supernatural power through prayer.

Here are two sides of a very important issue. Obviously, we must have willing minds in order to be the people God wants us to be. People who claim to be Christians but live in sin, do so basically because that is what they want to do. They like it. Living in sin is pleasurable and exciting for the present, and they are not looking beyond the present. They resent anyone telling them how God wants them to live. And until they have made up their minds to live holy lives, they will never change.

But deciding we want to change is not enough in itself. There is another aspect to this problem, as Christ's comment to His disciples makes perfectly clear. We simply do not have the power in ourselves to overcome temptation and live holy lives. We must claim that power from God through prayer, then act in conscious dependence on Him. That alone will lead to victory in Christian living.

But we cannot deny that the ability to live a godly life begins in the mind. That is probably why Peter began his exhortation to holy living by saying, "Wherefore, gird up the loins of your mind" (1 Peter 1:13, KJV; cf. vv. 13-16). People in Peter's day wore long flowing robes which hindered free movement. Before anyone did anything strenuous, he would lift the hem of his robe and tuck it into his belt. Then he would be "girded up" for action. Living a godly life is serious business, and if we are sincere about it, we will need to prepare our minds, gird up our minds for action, decide that we really want to do God's will, whatever it costs us. That is our decision to make. Are we willing to make it?

12
A Wise
Mind

The word *wise* often has a bad connotation in our culture. A wise guy is a cocky, conceited, know-it-all. A wiseacre is an interfering, overbearing smart aleck. A wisecrack is a flippant and unfeeling remark. With implications like that, it would not be surprising if we decided that *wise* was the last thing in the world we wanted to be.

Then we begin to read our Bibles, and God says, "Wisdom is supreme; therefore get wisdom. Though it cost all you have, get understanding" (Prov. 4:7, NIV). So God places a premium on wisdom. And when Solomon wanted to encourage and advise his son, he said, "My son, if your heart is wise, then my heart will be glad (Prov. 23:15, NIV). For his son to develop a wise heart would bring Solomon more joy than anything else he could think of, far more than attaining great wealth, fame, power, or influence. A wise heart is what I want for my children. But what is a wise heart, really?

There is no better place to begin learning what it is than in the Book of Proverbs. The words *wise* and *wisdom* occur well over 100 times in this book, and in a number of instances, they are directly related to the heart (or the *mind*, as the Hebrews used that term). In Proverbs, Solomon teaches us what it means to have a wise mind.

It Is Wise to Keep Ourselves Pure

There is a great deal of information in Proverbs about the right and wrong use of sex—what is wise and what is foolish. For example, "But whoso committeth adultery with a woman lacketh understanding; he that doeth it destroyeth his own soul" (Prov. 6:32, KJV). That word translated "understanding" is the Hebrew word for *heart* or *mind*. Quite literally, the person who commits adultery, who gets involved sexually outside marriage lacks a mind. He is out of his mind. He does not have any sense. He is not using good judgment. He has chosen a surefire way to ruin his life.

While the verse is addressed to the man (probably because he is most often the aggressor, the one on the prowl, who is looking for opportunities to satisfy his sexual desires), the same thing is true for a woman. It is just as stupid for her to commit adultery. And it is not uncommon for a lonely woman, hungry for companionship and affection, to set herself up for illicit sex by the situations she allows herself to get into, by the way she dresses, or merely by the flirtatious look in her eyes.

People who have been there know that what God says is true. They thought they had to get involved in order to meet some need in their lives. But committing adultery has destroyed them just as God said it would. It has brought a haunting and inescapable sense of guilt and shame. It has robbed them of their dignity and made them feel cheap and used. It has destroyed marriages and broken up homes. It has built suspicion and distrust. It has sabotaged satisfying sexual relationships within marriage. It has alienated people from each other and instigated conflicts. It has caused disease. It has given children a negative model to follow and an excuse to sin. It has ruined Christians' testimonies before the world. And all of that has been a high price to pay for a fleeting moment of pleasure. The people who choose impurity do not have wise minds.

I find it interesting that some of the same secular writers who promoted open marriages not long ago are now admitting that the most stable marriages are, in fact, based on fidelity, and that infidelity is a leading factor in causing broken homes. God said it thousands of years ago—a person who commits adultery is out of his mind; he destroys his life.

Of course, this principle is not only true for married people. Other passages in Proverbs warn unmarried people as well about getting involved sexually. One such passage begins with this call to wisdom: "Say to wisdom, 'You are my sister,' and call understanding your kinsman" (Prov. 7:4, NIV). After this passage follows the pathetic story of a young man who was not very wise. Solomon describes the scene: "At the window of my house I looked out through the lattice. I saw among the simple, I noticed among the young men, a youth who lacked judgment" (Prov. 7:6-7, NIV). That expression *lacked judgment* is the same one we just observed that means, literally, "lacking a mind." Here is somebody else who is out of his mind.

He is sauntering down the street, a little stuck-up, reasonably sure that he can handle any temptation without too much trouble. Suddenly, a woman approaches him and kisses him. (He always knew he was irresistible.) And when she describes all the alluring things she has waiting for him at home, he wilts. "With persuasive words she led him astray; she seduced him with her smooth talk. All at once he followed her like an ox going to the slaughter, like a deer stepping into a noose till an arrow pierces his liver, like a bird darting into a snare, little knowing it will cost him his life" (Prov. 7:21-23, NIV). It all sounds so exciting. And what could possibly be wrong with having a little fun? God says that the consequences of an episode like that could cost us our lives.

The evidence mounts as the book progresses. In chapter 9, Solomon describes a promiscuous woman sitting at the door of her house calling to those who pass by: " 'Whoever is naive, let him turn in here,' and to him who lacks understanding she says, 'Stolen water is sweet; and bread eaten in secret is pleasant.' But he does not know that the dead are there, that her guests are in the depths of Sheol" (Prov. 9:16-18). The man who responds to her overtures "lacks understanding." That is the same expression we have seen twice before. Such a man is missing his mind for all practical purposes. A wise person stays away from situations where the temptations he encounters are too great for him to handle.

Why are prohibitions regarding premarital and extramarital sex found in the Bible? Is it that God is a big ogre who wants to keep us from having fun? Certainly not. He simply knows how we are made, and He knows the principles that provide for the most efficient and satisfying operation of our lives. When we violate those established principles, we suffer mental, emotional, spiritual, and sometimes physical pain. And that is not being wise.

It Is Wise to Receive Instruction

People who are already involved in sexual sins probably do not like what I am pointing out here. Some may be rejecting it outright. Maybe they have always found it difficult to take advice from others and they resent anybody telling them how to live. That is not a very smart way to live. A wise person learns to receive instruction, to heed advice, and to accept biblical counsel.

"The wise in heart accept commands, but a chattering fool comes to ruin" (Prov. 10:8, NIV). A person with a wise mind is teachable. He hears what God says about his life and he happily subordinates himself to that higher Authority. He is in harmony with his Creator and, consequently, he is happy. But look at the fool by way of contrast. Solomon calls him a "chattering fool." Not only is he conceited and headstrong, refusing to listen to counsel and accept God's commands; he runs off at the mouth about it, trying to rationalize his behavior by telling everybody how ridiculous God's standards are. Things are going to get much worse for him. God says he will come to ruin.

A similar thought is repeated later: "He whose ear listens to the life-giving reproof will dwell among the wise. He who neglects discipline despises himself, but he who listens to reproof acquires understanding" (Prov. 15:31-32). Here the issue is reproof or correction. *Life-giving reproof* refers to an occasion when somebody shows us from the Word how God wants us to live and where we have departed from the Word, and then encourages us to come back to God's way. How do we respond to that? It depends on how smart we are. If we are wise, we accept it graciously and make the necessary changes. And in that case we acquire "understanding" (literally, *heart* or *mind*). You see, not only is it wise to accept reproof, but accepting it makes us even wiser.

This proverb also suggests that a person who rejects reproof does not think very highly of himself. He actually despises himself. That is a logical conclusion. If he willfully disobeys the Lord, and by that act puts himself in the divine woodshed (a place of discipline), he must not like himself very much. At least he certainly is not treating himself very kindly, and that is not very smart. When God deals with him through His Word, he needs to listen to what God says and obey it. He will be happier if he does.

It Is Wise to Work Diligently

Hard work is a major theme of the Book of Proverbs, linked consistently through the book to the wise mind. I realize *work* is a dirty word to some people, but Solomon lays it on the line. "Go to the ant, you sluggard; consider its ways and be wise! It has no commander, no overseer or ruler, yet it stores its provisions in summer and gathers its food at harvest. How long will you lie there, you sluggard? When will you get up from your sleep?" (Prov. 6:6-9, NIV)

We can learn a lesson about hard work by watching the ant. But as we know well, work for an ant is instinctive. For a human, willingness to work begins with a wise choice in the mind, and we can see the link between the two in this proverb: "He who works his land will have abundant food, but he who chases fantasies lacks judgment" (Prov. 12:11, NIV). "Lacks judgment" is that same Hebrew expression that refers to the missing mind. The person who spends his time chasing rainbows instead of working productively is out of his mind.

Recreation and relaxation are important. Scripture teaches that. But play has become an obsession in our culture. The "in" philosophy seems to be, "Work as little as you must to finance your favorite leisure time activities." And we let those activities gobble up vast amounts of time that could be used to serve the Lord, and inordinate amounts of money that could be used to reach a lost world with the Gospel of Jesus Christ.

A gullible public has now been informed that a certain sporting goods manufacturer "makes weekends." And all along I thought God made weekends, not just for recreation and relaxation, but to worship and serve Him. To get caught up in the philosophy of our day is not very smart. We may have a little fun over the weekend, but we will lose the only truly satisfying perspective about life that there is, as well as our reward in heaven. The person who pursues vain things is not using good judgment.

Once again Solomon wants to tell us about that fellow who doesn't have a brain in his head: "I went past the field of the sluggard, past the vineyard of the man who lacks judgment; thorns had come up everywhere, the ground was covered with weeds, and the stone wall was in ruins. I applied my heart to what I observed and learned a lesson from what I saw; a little sleep, a little slumber, a little folding of the hands to rest—and poverty will come on you like a bandit and scarcity like an armed man" (Prov. 24:30-34, NIV). Solomon seems to have some inside information on this man. He happens to know that this man is in on his couch taking a nap (or maybe watching television) when he should be out working in his vineyard. His wife is probably nagging him: "Abe, you better get that wall mended. And if you don't get those weeds pulled, we aren't going to have any grapes this year. Get up off that couch, you lazy good-for-nothing. My father told me I shouldn't have married you." But Abe snoozes on.

"Yeah, I'll get it done. Just give me a few more minutes."

But the minutes stretch into hours, and the hours into days, and the work never gets done.

That scene could be reenacted in 100 different ways in our own day. In some cases, the hero of the drama won't get up and go look for a job. In others, he is habitually late to work, or faking sickness. Poverty will come. He can count on it. And his marriage will probably fall apart, and his whole life may crumble while he snoozes on. He is not very smart. The wise man knows the meaning and value of hard work, and applies himself to it.

It Is Wise to Guard What We Say

The use of the tongue is another major theme of the Book of Proverbs, and again, it is linked to the wise mind. "A wise man's heart guides his mouth, and his lips promote instruction" (Prov. 16:23, NIV). We all know that what comes out of the mouth originates in the mind. Jesus verified that: "For out of the overflow of the heart the mouth speaks (Matt. 12:34, NIV). If there is wisdom in the mind, wisdom will come out of the mouth. If there is trivia in the mind, trivia will come out of the mouth.

Do you get a little troubled at times about what comes out of your mouth? We all do. Maybe we need to pay more attention to what we feed into our minds. Filling them with the wisdom of God's Word will serve as a guide and a guard over our lips. It will help us overcome the tendency to revert to our pre-conversion speech patterns, which in some cases were not very wholesome.

Solomon's exhortations to his son about a wise mind concern primarily his speech. "My son, if your heart is wise, then my heart will be glad; my inmost being will rejoice when your lips speak what is right (Prov. 23:15-16, NIV). He would be happy through and through if his son had a wise heart that led him to speak right things; that is, things that were true and honest, without distortion or deceit.

In a day of rampaging apostasy and false doctrine, we long for our children to speak God's truth courageously. It will largely depend on the degree to which they feed that truth into their minds. In a day of compromising ethics and crumbling morality, when lying is a way of life and getting caught is the only crime, we long for our children to be devoted steadfastly to truthfulness. Again it will largely depend on how faithfully they feed God's Word into their minds with understanding. Young people need to fill their minds with the Word. It will help them keep their mouths operating properly, speaking right things when others around them are spouting the foolish philosophy of the world.

Sometimes the wisest thing is to say nothing at all. "A fool gives full vent to his anger, but a wise man keeps himself under control" (Prov. 29:11, NIV). There is a time to speak, and a time to keep quiet (Ecc. 3:7), and a wise person has learned to discern which is which. The fool blurts out his angry words, hostile words, insulting words, cutting words, malicious words, and gossiping words. He cannot seem to control himself. But a wise person lets the Spirit of God master his emotions and muffle the words that breed contention or cause hard feelings.

Wisdom Alone Does Not Satisfy

Now we have seen a little of what true wisdom is and the importance God places on it. But I must be quick to add that wisdom alone will never satisfy us. Solomon told us that too. When he was invited to make a request from God, he asked for an understanding heart, a wise mind. God granted his request (1 Kings 3:9-12), and testified that Solomon was the wisest man in the East (1 Kings 4:29-34). The proverbs he gave us are evidence of his wisdom.

But Solomon himself said, "Then I applied myself to the understanding of wisdom . . . but I learned that this too is a chasing after the wind" (Ecc. 1:17, NIV). That is why God said through Jeremiah, " 'Let not the wise man boast of his wisdom . . . but let him who boasts boast about this; that he understands and knows Me, that I am the Lord, who exercises kindness, justice, and righteousness on the earth, for in these I delight,' declares the Lord" (Jer. 9:23-24, NIV). And that is why Solomon was led to say, "The fear of the Lord is the beginning of wisdom, and knowledge of the Holy One is understanding" (Prov. 9:10, NIV). The truest, purest, and most satisfying form of wisdom is simply knowing and adoring God. That should be the primary occupation of every wise-minded Christian. "So teach us to number our days, that we may apply our hearts unto wisdom (Ps. 90:12, KJV).

13
Molding the Mind

By now we should be convinced that what we feed into our minds could well be the most crucial aspect of establishing a happy, successful Christian life. Most of us want to feel good about our relationship with the Lord; we want to have warm feelings about His love and care, happy feelings over His personal presence in our lives, confident feelings about His sovereign control over every circumstance of life. But psychologists say that our feelings will be largely affected by our actions. And our actions, in turn, will be determined primarily by the way we think, by our mental perspective.

The Apostle Paul teaches us that our lives will be transformed, not by trying to develop certain kinds of feelings, but by renewing our minds (Rom. 12:2). If our mental computer is playing the right tape in any given situation, it is far more likely that we will do the right thing. And if we consistently do the right thing, we will begin to enjoy those good feelings we cherish so much. So we are back to the matter of what we program into our minds. The only way we can play the right tape at the right moment is, first of all, to have it in the computer. What we feed into our minds is the key to triumphant and joyful Christian living. One of the basic reasons for failure and defeat in our spiritual lives is that we neglect to program our minds with God's Word and bring our thoughts into conformity with His.

Maybe we neglect programming our minds with God's word because we do not know how do to it. It might be profitable to conclude our study of the mind by learning how to reprogram our thinking processes so that we can view life from God's perspective and make the choices that both please the Lord and bring us genuine satisfaction in living.

Take It In

It stands to reason that if we want the Word of God to mold our minds, we must first get it into our minds. We must have a daily intake of the Word. It is interesting to note that the authors of Scripture compare the reception of God's Word to eating. The Word itself is likened to food, such as meat, milk, bread, and honey; and appropriating the Word is like eating food (cf. Job 23:12; Jer. 15:16). So we need to have ourselves a feast. But how? There are several ways.

Hearing it taught. We should attend a church where we will get a good meal, where the pastor expounds, or explains, the Scripture and applies it to daily living. It is the responsibility of the shepherd to feed the sheep with God's Word. Ezra and the Levites performed that ministry to God's Old Testament sheep and thereby set a good example. "They read from the Book of the Law of God, making it clear and giving the meaning so the people could understand what was being read" (Neh. 8:8, NIV). We grow spiritually under that kind of ministry. So we must find a shepherd who feeds his sheep in order for us to have a spiritual feast.

Reading it personally. One meal a week is not enough, however. In fact, four meals are not enough (if we take in Sunday School, the Sunday evening service, and the midweek service as well). We need to do some eating on our own. We need to establish a program of daily Bible reading, set a regular time for it, and then organize our lives around it. If we just try to fit Bible reading in when we have the time, we will seldom do it. Bible reading needs to be as important as eating, and we need to do it as regularly as we eat our meals. Unless we approach it with that attitude, we may live our entire lives on good intentions alone.

Studying it. Just reading will not be enough, however. We must understand the meaning of what we are reading, and that requires study. If there is something we do not understand, we should not skip over it. Rather, we need to study it through; consult an English dictionary, a Bible dictionary, a Bible encyclopedia, a concordance, a Bible atlas, reference notes, commentaries, books on Bible doctrine, word studies, and other helps.

And we shouldn't read into the passage what we want it to mean. Rather, we need to find out what God meant when He said it. Some unusual things have been derived from the Bible in the guise of "getting a blessing." The Bible must speak for itself.

Memorizing it. Hearing, reading, and studying are all necessary elements of building the Word into our minds. But none of them will help us recall the Word when we need it as much as this fourth element will. The Word needs to be committed to memory. When that unexpected bill comes in, or that irritating interruption shatters our schedule, or that devastating news of a terminal illness first strikes our ears, there may be no Bible within reach. We need to have God's truth permanently stored in our minds so that we can call it to remembrance.

Scripture itself encourages us to memorize. "Accept instruction form His mouth and lay up His words in your heart" (Job 22:22, NIV). "I have hidden Your Word in my heart that I might not sin against You" (Ps. 119:11, NIV). "Let the Word of Christ dwell in you richly" (Col. 3:16, KJV). Let it settle down and be at home in you abundantly. Be comfortable with it. Let it make its valuable contribution to your life. Fix it firmly in your mind, assimilate it into your storehouse of knowledge, make it a permanent addition to your memory bank. To do less may be like tasting food and then spitting it out again.

A few of you will protest, "But I can't memorize. I'm too

young, or too old, or too busy, or too dumb." That's non-sense! You can remember your street address, zip code, and telephone number, can't you? Do you know why you remember those things? Because of *repetition!* And the same principle can help you remember God's Word. Write it on a small card. Carry it with you when you go out. Tape it on the bathroom mirror. Learn one phrase at a time; repeat it over and over. Whenever you find a spare minute, repeat it again. The key to memorization is review, review, and more review. Anyone can do it. And if you want your spiritual life to prosper, you will do it.

Chew It Up

Now that we have fed the necessary spiritual food into our minds, there is a second important step to renewing the mind with God's thoughts. God wants us to meditate on the Scriptures we have memorized (cf. Josh. 1:8; Ps. 1:2). The Hebrew word *meditate* (*hagah*) has the basic idea of muttering. It pictures someone mentally searching, deep in thought, turning something over in his mind, even mumbling to himself about it. Some have likened the meaning of this Hebrew word to an animal chewing the cud. While the Hebrew word does not actually have that meaning, it is a helpful analogy. An English synonym for *meditate* is *ruminate,* and that word is used to refer to an animal that chews its cud. It is called a ruminant animal. This animal consumes a great amount of food rapidly, stores it in a separate stomach compartment, then lies down in the shade and rechews the food thoroughly bit by bit before swallowing it, digesting it, and absorbing it into the bloodstream. The ruminating or chewing of the cud prepares the food to become part of the animal's body.

When we meditate on the Word, we chew on it, mutter it to ourselves, muse on it, ponder it, and mull it over in our minds. We also digest the Word, extract spiritual nourishment from it, and absorb it into the bloodstream of our spiritual lives where it becomes part of us. We turn the truth over and over in our minds, then allow it to sift into our memories and consciences where the Holy Spirit of God can use it to guide our choices, empower our actions, and remodel our behavior. When our minds are saturated with God's mind as revealed in the Word, we can think as He thinks and view things as He sees them— and that is crucial to a happy, successful Christian life.

If we were to read books by the same author every day over a long period of time, or talk to the same person in depth day after day, eventually we would begin to think like that person. The Bible is God's Word. He is speaking to us in its pages. If we let His thoughts occupy our minds day after day, we will grow in His likeness and begin to view life from His perspective. That brings inner peace, which leads to increased effectiveness, which results in greater success and happiness. Things go better when we meditate on God's Word. So let us see how it is done. There are three basic elements to spiritual ruminating.

Analyzing the meaning. In our study time, we have determined generally what the passage means; but now we want to examine it more closely, see the nature of its separate parts, and their relationship to each other. We are going to take the verse apart piece by piece, look at the pieces individually, consider their implications, think through their connection to each other, then put the verse back together again. We will want to consider questions like who, what, when, where, why, and how. Suggesting answers to our questions will bring us into a deeper understanding of the meaning.

Memorizing words that have no meaning will be of little value to us. A parakeet can repeat words, but to my knowledge it doesn't have much of a spiritual life. True meditation is not emptying our minds of all conscious thoughts. It is focusing our thoughts on a specific object so as to understand it more completely.

Suppose, for example, you have recently memorized those great words of our Lord Jesus in John 10:27: "My sheep hear My voice, and I know them, and they follow Me." Now you're lying in bed thinking before you drop off to sleep, or you're walking to the store, or cutting the grass, or ironing the clothes—all of which are ideal times to meditate on the words you have committed to memory. And you are thinking about that verse word by word: "My"—*I belong to the Lord Jesus; I am His.* "Sheep"—*why does God call me His sheep? What characteristics should I have that resemble sheep?* "Hear"—*He communicates with His sheep and He wants them to listen. I would probably rather talk than listen, but I am ready to listen to what God has to say to me through His Word.* "My voice"—*what does the Shepherd's voice mean to the sheep? What is the voice of Christ? How does He speak to me today?*

As you think through questions like these, and answers begin to dawn on your consciousness, you will find yourself thinking more and more as God thinks, and become capable of looking at life from His perspective. And you can chew on just about any portion from the Bible like that.

Pondering the application. As you analyze the meaning of the verse, you will also want to be thinking through its various applications to your life. In other words, what does this passage mean to me? What difference should it make in my life? What should I be thinking, what ought I to be saying, and how does God want me to be acting in the light of this verse? Here are some specific areas of application to consider when meditating on God's Word: an action to take, an attitude to develop, a command to obey, an error to avoid, an example to follow, a matter for prayer, a promise to believe, a sin to confess and forsake, a truth to enjoy, or a warning to heed.

Now go back to your meditation on John 10:27 for a moment. "My sheep hear My voice, and I know them." "I know them"—*what a fantastic truth! The Lord knows me in a unique, personal, saving relationship, in a special, intimate friendship. He knows all about me—my weaknesses, my failures, and my sins. He knows what a stubborn sheep I am. Yet He loves me, accepts me, and cares for me anyway. What a wonderful Saviour!* "And they follow Me"—*are there areas in my life where I am not following my Shepherd closely enough? How about His unselfish concern for others? I really didn't express much concern for my neighbor who lost a loved one last week. I need to show him Christ's love, and by God's grace I will do it.*

It might be profitable to get a pencil and paper at an opportune time and write down what God has impressed on you to do and the changes He has asked you to make. Read back over them periodically and check up on your spiritual progress. If you do that consistently, you can be sure there will be growth in your life.

Responding with worship. It is impossible to ponder the great truths of God's Word without developing deep feelings of love and gratitude to Him. So express those thoughts in prayer and praise. Let your meditation about Him lead you into direct communion with Him. Thank Him for who He is and what He has done for you. Quote what you have learned back to Him in praise. From John 10:27, for example, you have learned about Christ's omniscience. He knows you. *Lord, You are wonderful. You know me, and You love me anyway. Thank You for the immensity of Your love and for the faithfulness of Your care to one of the least of Your sheep.* Then mention those matters for prayer that were brought to your attention through the Word, and enjoy a meaningful and precious time of communion with the Lord.

Live It Out

Now it is time to translate the truth which the Spirit of God has etched on our minds into concrete action. We have begun to develop new perspectives, new priorities, and new purposes as we have meditated on the Word. Now we must determine to follow through with new confidence and conviction and put that truth into daily practice. The response God wants is not just knowledge, but obedience. And the Bible never suggests that it will be easy to obey. We may not feel like doing what God wants us to do. We may not feel like visiting that neighbor, for example. We would rather stay home and relax. We may not feel like treating our spouse with tenderness and kindness after that blowup between us. We would rather sulk for awhile. We may not want to accept a tragedy with thanksgiving. We would rather complain. We may not want to believe that our sovereign, loving Lord is in control of our circumstances and will work them out for good. We would rather feel sorry for ourselves.

That is when we need to go back to the truth we have learned through memorization and meditation and play it over again in our minds. Then we must consciously, willfully choose to act in accord with the Word, depending on the power which the Spirit of God provides. That is how we grow. That is how we attain new heights of victory, joy, and blessing. God promises those exciting benefits as a direct result of meditating on His Word and obeying it. Some of those promises need to be considered.

The first one was given to Joshua shortly after the death of Moses. God had commissioned Joshua to take Moses' place and to lead the chosen people in the conquest of their Promised Land. It was an awesome responsibility! They were greatly outnumbered by powerful enemies. How could Joshua be sure the campaign would succeed? "Do not let this Book of the Law depart from your mouth; meditate on it day and night, so that you may be careful to do everything written in it. Then you will be prosperous and successful" (Josh. 1:8, NIV). Success would not come by building bigger and better weapons systems, by staying up all night for strategy sessions, or by moving through the ranks giving inspiring pep talks to his men. It would come by meditating on the Word of God and by doing what it said. What an incredible promise! To be prosperous meant that Joshua would succeed in what he was called to do. To be successful actually meant that he would act wisely. By meditating on God's Word, Joshua would know the wise thing to do, the thing that would bring him the achievement, accomplishment, and success that God wanted him to have.

The next such promise comes through the inspired psalmist: "Blessed is the man who does not walk in the counsel of the wicked or stand in the way of sinners or sit in the seat of mockers. But his delight is in the Law of the Lord, and on His Law he meditates day and night. He is like a tree planted by streams of water, which yields its fruit in season and whose leaf does not wither. Whatever he does prospers" (Ps. 1:1-3, NIV). These verses describe a happy person. That is what the word *blessed* means. The happy person does not take counsel from ungodly men, but rather from God's Word. He delights in it and meditates on it day and night. He mulls it over in his mind and enjoys following its advice.

And look at the results. He is like a tree beside streams of water. There is stability in his life. Nothing shakes him. He draws deeply on the resources which God continually supplies. And he brings forth fruit. The fruit of a tree is produced by nourishment over and above what is required to sustain life and produce growth. It is the product of excess life, the over and above, the added dimension. Fruit is the life of the tree at its best. So the fruitful Christian has that added dimension in his life; he enjoys life at its best—peace, joy, satisfaction, and abundant living. Furthermore, his leaf does not wither. There is a steadfastness about him. Even when the dry spells come, he keeps right on producing. And everything he puts his hand to, within the will of God, enjoys the success God wants it to have.

A third such promise was made through the Apostle Paul to Timothy. Paul was referring to Timothy's relationship to the Scriptures when he said, "Meditate upon these things; give thyself wholly to them, that thy profiting may appear to all" (1 Tim. 4:15 KJV). This particular word translated "meditate" can mean "to take pains with" or "to give diligence to." But it can also mean "to think about, meditate on, or ponder." Paul seems to be using it in that latter sense here, consistent with the Old Testament concepts we have just seen. If Timothy would keep on thinking about the doctrines of the Word and their application to his life, his spiritual progress would be obvious to all. People would see the blessing of God on his life.

James promised much the same thing: "But the man who looks intently into the perfect Law that gives freedom, and continues to do this, not forgetting what he has heard, but doing it—he will be blessed in what he does" (James 1:25 NIV). The word *meditate* does not appear in this verse, but the same process is graphically depicted. To *look intently* is to stoop down beside and take a long, careful look. And the person James is describing continues to let the truth of God's Word linger in his mind. That is a beautiful explanation of meditation. And it is followed by obedience; he practices what the Word says. We are not surprised to see that the result is *blessing*—spiritual success and genuine joy.

It almost sounds too good to be true, doesn't it? Yet it is genuinely offered to us by the unchanging God who inspired this infallible Word. These wondrous benefits are available to us if we will feed on God's Word daily, meditate on it regularly so that it molds our minds into His thought patterns, and then obey it faithfully to His glory. Our lives will be transformed as our minds are renewed. What keeps us from enjoying these blessings? Let's make up our minds to feed and mediate on God's word and then obey it.